SOAP OPERAS OF THE SKY

Your Tropical Vacation Stargazing
Story Guide To Dancing Coyotes,
Greedy Crows And Messy Objects

With Sta᠁ ᠁ ᠁ Down To
Twelve Degrees Nᴖᵣ ᠁ atitude.

by
JEANNIE KUICH

D1114604

SOAP OPERAS OF THE SKY

Your Tropical Vacation Stargazing
Story Guide To Dancing Coyotes,
Greedy Crows And Messy Objects

With Star Charts Down To
Twelve Degrees North Latitude.

Ad Astra per Aspera
By striving, you will reach the stars

To
Mike
the Sun of my universe
who didn't complain when I bought
the largest telescope he could carry

Library of Congress Cataloging in Publication Data
Kuich, Jeannie
  Soap Operas of the Sky
    (Your Stargazing Story Guide to Dancing Coyotes,
    Greedy Crows, & Messy Objects with Star Charts to
    Twelve Degrees North Latitude)

              CIP
          93-073786

ISBN 0-944428-23-1
Published 1994

Preface

*W*elcome to the sky video screen. The soap operas of the sky rival those seen on Earth. Tonight you may see Corvus the Greedy Crow who forgot Apollo's Heineken, or witness the rescue of Cepheus's teenaged daughter, Andromeda, by Perseus the Hero on his hang-glider. This guide includes stories and charts of the whole sky as well as the southern constellations, which you may never have seen until you entered the tropics. The four sections are divided by season and the constellations are explored in accordance with the dramas that group them together. Some of these stories are modernized and more than one version may be included.

This guide is dedicated to you, the skygazer, who may look at the heavens at first with bewilderment and then with delight as you become enchanted with the gods and goddesses, beasts and dragons in the sky. As you read about their adventures and learn their destinies, you may discover dazzling celestial treasures that you may log in your paper treasure chest at the end of each section.

If ours had been the first civilization to place figures in the sky that were significant to our lives, we would surely have such constellations as the Motorcycle, the Sports Car, the Refrigerator, the Computer, etc. By learning the sky patterns of the ages and modernizing them with clever patterns of your own, you may make the sky a familiar home.

Eons ago there weren't any stars in the sky to look at until Streak the Dancing Coyote came along. Now what does a dumb coyote have to do with the sky? Well, according to many native Americans, it all started when . . . Oh! Oh! You're not supposed to hear this story yet! Please read the Introduction first.

Acknowledgments

cknowledgments can be boring to read, but this adventure could not have been accomplished without the support, help and advice of other people. Bear with me while I thank all my family and friends who contributed so lovingly to this project. In particular, special thanks go to: Mike for his patience and letting me type instead of varnish; Kevin Foley and Marvin and Carol Jacoby for their enthusiasm and encouragement; Diane Delorey for her delightful sketch of Streak the Dancing Coyote; Mike Klatka for his charming illustrations; Fatty Goodlander and Fritz Seyfarth for their invaluable advice; Henry Holzkamper and Jan Moore for their generosity, spending hours instructing me on their computers; Bud Beaulieu for his friendly electricity, table and chair; the Virgin Islands Charteryacht League for its facilities, the folks behind TheSky program at Software Bisque upon which the charts are based and the staff at Cruising Guide Publications.

Table of Contents

I
Helios, the Sun God
1

II
The Moon—The Basket Woman
3

III
The Milky Way—Big White Trail
5

IV
Falling Stars—Dancing Coyotes
9

V
Winter Sky Preview
11

VI
The Winter Obscure Constellations
42

VII
Spring Sky Preview
46

X
The Summer Obscure Constellations
115

XI
Autumn Sky Preview
118

XII
The Autumn Obscure Constellations
150

Introduction

*I*t is dusk and the last golden rays of the Sun have kissed the lagoon good night. Alone in his log canoe the solitary figure skillfully plies his paddle toward the pale horizon, leaving his family and his village behind. Silently he glides around the coral heads, negotiates the slender pass through the reef, and as he meets the ocean's first mighty swell, his bow lifts, then plunges into seething foam, the spray bathing his face. As the tropical dusk darkens swiftly into blackness, a brilliant star blinks and beckons him across the ocean to a distant land. He has cut his ties, left behind all he has ever owned and he has ventured forth, brave and fearless to challenge the vast waters in search of—cigarettes!

Perhaps early seafarers followed a bright star such as Sirius or Vega for other reasons, but no matter. This is how it might have happened and that bright star could have been named and revered because it guided the sailor to the next land or the desert nomad across the sands to life-giving waterholes. Or perhaps the appearance of a certain group of stars signaled to farmers that it was time to plant or harvest. To pass the long dark nights and to try to explain the phenomenon around him, early man invented stories and transferred them to the sky. The constellations were not created to literally resemble the characters in the myths they represent but only to symbolize them. The stories came first and the star patterns representing them came later.

The originators of the constellations that we use are believed to have been the Sumerians, ancestors of the Babylonians who occupied Mesopotamia, known today as Iraq, about 4000 B.C. The Greek astronomer Eudoxus (c. 390–340 B.C.) learned of the constellations from the priests in Egypt and he is considered to be the first to introduce them to Greece. His descriptions of the constellations in his *Phaenomena* were lost, but his work was commemorated in a poem by the same name by another Greek, Aratus (c. 315–245 B.C.). Around A.D. 150 forty-eight constellations were identified and summarized in a catalogue of 1022 stars called the *Almagest* and compiled by the Greek astronomer Claudius Ptolemy (c. A.D. 100—c. 178) when he worked in Alexandria, Egypt. Ptolemy's constellation system, although modified extensively, still remains the same with the exception of Argo Navis that was later subdivided.

After Ptolemy mapmakers of Europe and Arabia gradually added names to the stars, but it wasn't until approximately 1500 years later that additional constellations were invented. Crux, the Southern Cross, one of the prominent constellations of the southern sky, was probably one of the first of these to be recognized, although the Greeks knew it as the hind legs of Centaurus the Centaur. The Italian navigator Andraes Cossali seems to have been the originator of Crux when he described it so enthusiastically in 1516. In 1551 the Dutch cartographer Gerardus Mercator depicted Coma Berenices and toward the end of the 16th century, the Dutch navigators Pieter Dvikszoor Keyser and Friderick de Houtman are thought to have introduced twelve new constellations and compiled a catalogue of 135 stars. Another three constellations were introduced by the Dutch cartographer Petrus Plancius that were formed from some of the fainter uncharted stars sprinkled between established constellations. The Polish astronomer Johannes Hevelius (1611–1687) filled in the still existing gaps of the northern sky with seven more constellations, bringing the count to 71.

Now that the northern sky was sufficiently complete, Nicolas Louis de Lacaille (1713–1762), a French astronomer, filled the vacant holes in the southern sky. From a site near the Cape of Good Hope in South Africa he subdivided Argo Navis into three separate constellations—Carina the Keel, Puppis the Stern and Vela the Sail—and added fourteen more, most of which commemorate scientific instruments.

This total brought the number of constellations to eighty-eight. A few more were stuck in here and there, but they were discarded. In 1928 the International Astronomical Union officially adopted the eighty-eight constellations and commissioned the Belgian astronomer Eugene Delporte (1882–1955) to draw up the boundaries of the constellations. Since many of the later constellations are faint and hard to see easily, they are mostly included under the Obscure Constellations chapter at the end of each season.

All the stars that we see are part of our Milky Way Galaxy. About two thousand of them are visible at one time to our naked eye when sky conditions are excellent. If you are among the thousands of visitors who come to the tropics for a vacation, you may realize that you are seeing much more of the southern sky than you can from your home in the northern latitudes. Although the eastern and western sections are identical to those in the more northern latitudes, the northern and southern sections are different. In the tropics we see less of the northern sky and Polaris, the North Star, is much lower than in the United States. Most of Ursa Major and Ursa Minor, the Great and Little Bears, dip below the tropical horizon whereas in the north, the Bears circle the North Pole without getting their feet wet!

In the southern sky some of the constellations that you see in the tropics such as Crux, the famous Southern Cross, and Pavo the Peacock are below your home horizon. If you know the latitude upon which you live, subtract the latitude where you are now from your latitude at home and the difference will equal the additional section of the southern sky you can see.

The sets of four charts for each season depict the sky from 12 degrees north latitude and are useful for latitudes approximately up to 45 degrees north. The other charts illustrate the constellations in family groups according to the legends that connect them or because they lie adjacent to one another. The charts represent the sky at 9:00 p.m. local daylight time and may apply one hour before and after nine o'clock. If you stargaze in the wee hours of the morning, then consult the charts for the next season.

All charts have been computed from TheSky Astronomy Software copyrighted 1992 and adapted for the horizon at 12 degrees north. Spherical projections are used to minimize distortion of the constellations. Stars are shown to magnitude 8.0 as are selected deep-sky objects such as galaxies, star clusters and nebulae. The dotted lines indicate the path of the Milky Way.

To use a chart turn it so the direction you are facing is at the bottom of the chart. The sky moves 15 degrees each hour, so constellations that rose in the east in the early evening will be upside down when they descend in the west before dawn. if you should rise before morning twilight and look toward the east, you will see the stars of the following season appearing, making a preview of the next soap opera.

No planets have been plotted on the charts because they are always moving along the ecliptic, the imaginary plane in the sky marked by the twelve constellations in the Zodiac through which the Sun and the planets appear to move. The Chinese called their Zodiac the Yellow Road.

Venus, the brightest planet, is six times brighter than Sirius, the brightest star. Venus is never more than 45 degrees from the Sun either in the west after sunset or in the east before sunrise. Jupiter, which is almost twice as bright as Sirius, takes roughly twelve months to travel once around the ecliptic. This motion may account for the creation of the twelve signs of the Zodiac. With binoculars the four brightest moons of Jupiter may be seen in a straight line on either side of the planet in different positions each night. Mars is distinctly yellow-orange compared to Venus and Jupiter while Saturn is a creamy golden. If you see a relatively stationary bright object in the sky that doesn't appear on the charts, you are looking at a planet.

Distances between the stars and planets from your view on Earth are difficult to gauge unless you use a measure of some sort. The handiest ruler is the one you always carry with you—your hand. The width of your little pinkie, when held at arm's length, is just under one degree. The three middle fingers equal roughly five degrees and the full width of your hand is about ten degrees. To test your ruler, look at the two pointer stars, Dubhe (Alpha Ursae Majoris) and Merak (Beta Ursae Majoris) in the Big Dipper. Your three fingers will just fit between them, so Dubhe and Merak are five degrees apart.

Time now to turn off the lights, find a cool one and prop your feet up in the cockpit of your yacht or perhaps the deck chair of your ship, hotel balcony, or backyard. The tools you need to watch the sky video are few. A red-lensed flashlight for reading the charts is a must. If you can't find anything red to put over the lense, a brown paper bag will do. A pair of binoculars, preferably 7x50s, is a superb asset to assist your peepers. Have a pen or pencil ready to log the sky jewels that you find in your paper treasure chest. And lastly, have a happy and inventive imagination. If you have trouble tracing the constellations which, in many instances, hardly resemble what their names suggest, create asterisms, easy to recognize patterns such as triangles, circles or whatever figure helps you to navigate through the magnificent night sky.

Helios, The Sun God

*A*mong the cast of billions on the sky screen, none is more important to us than the Earth's own star, the Sun. Appropriately we'll begin our acquaintance of the sky drama with a modernized version of the catastrophic adventure of Phaethon, the son of Helios, described in *Metamorphoses* by the Roman poet Ovid.

In the days of the Roman Empire the Sun God Helios was the supreme deity. One day Phaethon, the son of Helios, was spitefully challenged by a jealous friend to prove his ancestry. In some doubt, Phaethon approached his magnificent father, and holding a hand in front of his eyes to block out the dazzling brilliance, haltingly asked Helios for the truth. Helios assured Phaethon that he was indeed his son and to show his love for him, promised to grant Phaethon anything he wished. Phaethon was a cool cat and told his dad that his only desire was to drive the Sun Chariot, the gleaming, white, souped-up 400 horsepower Lambourghini convertible, across the sky for one day. Helios was horrified. He knew the boy would be unable to control the car, but he couldn't refuse him. Reluctantly, Helios granted Phaethon's wish and explained how to use the gears and brakes and the best techniques for driving the Heavenly Road.

"Do not take the direct road through the Five Zones of the sky, but cut obliquely in a wide arc within the Three Zones, skirting South Heaven and Far North."

Of course, Phaethon ignored his advice and took off in a flat-out drag. Burning rubber around the first curve, he lost control and plunged erratically across the sky, coming so close to Earth that he scorched it. Smoldering and in agony, Gaia, the Mother Earth, appealed to Jupiter, King of the Deities, to stop the chariot. Jupiter ignored her pleas until Phaethon narrowly missed colliding with Venus and Mercury. No longer able to stand the roaring of the loud, powerful engine and the screeching of the tires, Jupiter hurtled a thunderbolt and blew out a tire. When Phaethon braked, the Sun Chariot swerved off the Heavenly Road and Phaethon was thrown from the car. He fell to Earth and drowned in the River Eridanus. The Lambourghini smashed against an asteroid and disintegrated into a thousand pieces, which caused a meteor shower. The Heavenly Road, marred by great streaks of black tire marks, then became the Milky Way.

* * * * *

The Sun is a middle-aged star, a type G yellow dwarf. The term dwarf refers to the classification of a star, not to its size. In this sense the Sun has not yet evolved into a supergiant such as Betelgeuse (Alpha Orionis) or Antares (Alpha Scorpii) which you will meet later.

The diameter of the Sun is one million miles and it weighs 700 times that of the combined weight of the nine planets. In a few billion years, after it has converted its hydrogen into a helium core, it will become ruddy and bloated and destroy all life on Earth.

II

The Moon —
The Basket Woman

Although the Moon, our lone satellite, is not a star, she is a frequent feature of the sky. She has the important role as the Mother of the Stars and the sister of Helios, the Sun God.

To the Skidi, a tribe belonging to the Pawnee Indians of North America, the Moon was the Basket Woman because during the creation, the Sun used her to carry the stars to Earth. These stars, who were the children of Basket Woman, were brought to Earth to teach the First Man and First Woman everything that people of the Earth were to do. After they learned all they should, the stars jumped back into the Moon Basket and went back into the sky.

As Selene in the Greek myth, she is a beautiful woman who is charmed by Jupiter and becomes the mother of three daughters by him. Their escapades were discovered by Jupiter's wife, Juno, and even though Jupiter changed Selene into a white heifer, Juno was not thwarted. She placed the heifer under the guard of Argus, the giant with one hundred eyes that symbolize the stars. Selene was made to wander night after night among the stars in different constellations and was finally rescued when Mercury,

3

the Messenger of the Gods, killed Argus. Just as his one hundred eyes closed in death, so dim the stars as dawn approaches.

Where is the Man in the Moon? The Man in the Moon is made up of the bright and dark areas which sometimes resemble a human face. A German fable tells us that the Old Man in the Moon was once a villager who stole some cabbages from his neighbor. He was punished by being banished to the inhospitable Moon. People in the southern latitudes see a rabbit in the Moon, whose head and long, narrow ears project into the large, bright area.

The Moon is a barren world pocked with craters, but she is a stunning beauty in all her phases and is unquestionably the Queen of the Night. It is no wonder that the ancients worshipped her as a radiant goddess clothed in silver robes, crowned by a luminous tiara, sweeping across the sky in her chariot pulled by magnificent white stallions.

* * * * *

The most prominent features of the Moon are the large, grey lava plains which are called seas, even though there was never any water in them. Huge craters pock the surface, from nearly 150 miles in diameter to invisible pits. Two craters, Copernicus and Tycho, each over 50 miles in diameter, appear as bright white spots to the naked eye. Clavius, nearly 150 miles across, is discernible when it is near the terminator, the line between the dark and lit hemispheres of the Moon.

When the Moon appears as a crescent, emerging into the twilight, the most noticeable plain is the Mare Crisium (Sea of Crises) which is the small, oval-shaped spot near the edge. After the Full Moon phase, the Mare Crisium disappears first. While a crescent, the dark part of the Moon is weakly illuminated by Earthshine, light reflected from the Sun, so that it can easily be seen. Then, it is said, the Old Moon is held in the New Moon's arms.

The Milky Way —
Big White Trail

The glory of the sky screen is the Milky Way, a great girdle of doubloons, diamonds, rubies, sapphires and other gems that wrap around the belly of the sky. Before you hear the tales of the constellations, pause here for the rich legends that abound about this gleaming silver stream.

Throughout ancient civilizations the Milky Way has been seen as a passageway, a road, and a river or bridge for souls of the dead to travel from the Earth to Heaven. Hunting clans believed the sky was a great bear skin with holes in it through which the camp fires of other hunters shone through.

Some American Indians believed the Milky Way was the Circular Cord of Silver Feathers. The Eskimo and Bushmen of Africa called it the Ashen Path with glowing coals. Reflecting their dependence on fishing, the Polynesians called it the Long, Blue Cloud-Eating Shark. Others, such as the Norsemen, knew it as the Pathway of the Ghosts.

An unusual, humorous myth comes from the Cherokee tribe, who called it Where The Dog Ran. During the time when they used to grind corn into a fine, white meal, the women, one early morning, found a lot of cornmeal scattered on the ground. They saw dog tracks in the cornmeal and decided to ambush the culprit that night if he returned. Shortly after midnight a large dog from the north ran straight to the mill and started eating. The women sprang up and chased the dog, beating him with a stick. As he ran away howling, the cornmeal spilled from his mouth, leaving a milky white trail which became scattered across the sky.

A Greek story involves Hercules, son of Jupiter and Alemene, a mortal woman. Jupiter secretly placed his newborn son beside his wife Juno while she was sleeping so that the baby would suckle her godly breasts and thus achieve immortality. The sturdy child suckled so powerfully that much of the magic milk was spilt and sprayed over the heavens. This spray formed the Milky Way and the stray drops which landed on the Earth became the flowers known as lilies.

A native American story tells us that one evening a mischievous coyote went to Black God's camp fire. When Black God wasn't looking, Coyote stole his pouch which contained most of the stars. There weren't many placed in the sky yet so Coyote started arranging the stars in pretty patterns which became the constellations. Coyote soon tired of this tedious job and threw all the stars up at once into the sky. Many of them concentrated into globs in a wide band which became the Big White Trail and the rest were scattered all over the sky.

* * * * *

The name Milky Way comes from the Greek word *gala*, meaning milk. The Milky Way is part of our galaxy, a disk-shaped spiral with a diameter of at least 100,000 light years.[1] The Sun, with its planets, lies near the Orion arm about 20,000 light years from its edge. When you look at the Milky Way, you are gazing toward the center of the galaxy which is composed of layers and layers of billions of stars. Dark clouds of gas and dust block much of the

Milky Way. Two of the most famous of these nebulous masses are the Great Rift which clefts the Milky Way from Cygnus to the southern sky and the Coal Sack, tucked beside the east side of Crux, the Southern Cross.

Phaethon and the Sun Chariot
Careening Across the Sky

IV

Falling Stars — Dancing Coyotes

*F*alling stars or shooting stars — what are they? This charming tale from the native Americans of the Pacific northwest and the Plateau area has one explanation.

A very long time ago, Streak was an ordinary Earthbound coyote except for one thing. He loved to dance from dusk until dawn. One night Streak saw the stars dancing above him and thought, "I sure wish I could go up there. Maybe they would let me dance with them."

The next silvery night — the Moon was dancing too — Streak called up to the stars and asked them if he could come up and dance with them.

"No way," said a pretty little star. "You'll get tired and fall back to Earth." "Oh, but I won't!" cried Streak. "I'm big and strong! Please let me come up and dance with you!"

The stars finally consented and told Streak that if he could find his way up to the sky, he could dance with them. Streak thought and thought. He decided to make an arrow ladder. First he gathered many arrows together and shot one arrow into the sky, where it stuck. The second arrow struck the shaft of the first arrow and stayed. So did the third arrow that Streak shot at the second arrow. Pretty

9

soon a long ladder of arrows grew until it touched the ground. Streak climbed on it past the shimmering Moon who winked at him as he went by, past the Silver Stream — the Milky Way — and on to the kingdom of the stars. There Streak began to dance each night for millions of years. Zip, Zing and Whiz, his coyote buddies on Earth, saw Streak dancing and wanted to come up too. After seeing how great a dancer Streak was, the stars permitted his friends to join him.

Occasionally, after a hundred million years or so, one of them would get too tired and down he would fall. When you see a falling star, it may be one of these dancing coyotes maybe, Zip or Zing, too weary to dance anymore. Sometimes, lots of dancing coyotes fall down at the same time, making meteor showers.[2]

Streak the Dancing Coyote
by Diane Delorey

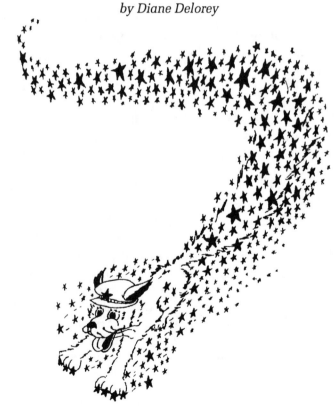

V

Winter Sky Preview

*I*f the stargazer could choose only one of the four seasonal sky videos, he would probably select the winter. The cooler air is usually clearer so that the stars stand out boldly, dressed up in their best bib and tucker. More stars of first magnitude[3] abound in the winter sky than in any other. Among the brightest are the fiery diamonds Sirius, Procyon and Canopus; the sapphires, Rigel and Achernar; the rubies, Betelgeuse, Aldebaran and Pollux; and the topaz, Capella.

Some of the most beautiful brooches, the star clusters, are found in the winter sky. The most famous are M45, the Pleiades known as the Seven Sisters, and the Hyades, their half sisters, both in Taurus the Bull. Other equally exquisite clusters are M35 near Castor's big toe in Gemini the Twins, M41 about four degrees south of Sirius in Canis Major, the Great Dog, and NGC-4755, the Jewel Box beside Crux, the Southern Cross.

The crowning gem of the northern sky is M42, the Orion Nebula within Orion the Giant Hunter's dagger. Near the southern horizon in Dorado, the Gold Fish is the Large Magellanic Cloud — a glowing misty patch. It is the larger of the two satellite galaxies that orbit our Milky Way Galaxy. These jewels and many others await your jeweler's glass — your binoculars — or your eye alone.

WINTERTIME SKY LOOKING NORTH

NGC Objects:
- Galaxy
- Open Cluster
- Global Cluster
- Planetary Nebula
- Nebula
- Cluster + Nebulosity
- Star
- Other NGC Objects
- Milky Way

Stars:
- 9.5 • 5.0
- 9.0 • 4.5
- 8.0 • 3.8
- 7.5 • 3.1
- 7.0 • 2.8
- 6.0 • 2.5
- 5.6 • 2.0
- 5.3 • 1.0

The Sky Astronomy Software © 1992

The horizon is at 12° North Latitude for January 1st..

12

WINTERTIME SKY LOOKING EAST

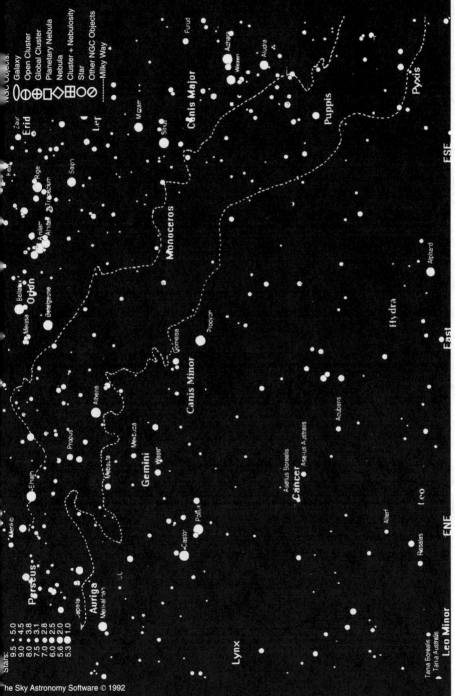

Stars:

9.5	5.0
9.0	4.5
8.0	3.8
7.5	3.1
7.0	2.8
6.0	2.5
5.6	2.0
5.3	1.0

NGC Objects:
- Galaxy
- Open Cluster
- Global Cluster
- Planetary Nebula
- Nebula
- Cluster + Nebulosity
- Star
- Other NGC Objects
- Milky Way

The Sky Astronomy Software © 1992

The horizon is at 12° North Latitude for January 1st.

WINTERTIME SKY LOOKING SOUTH

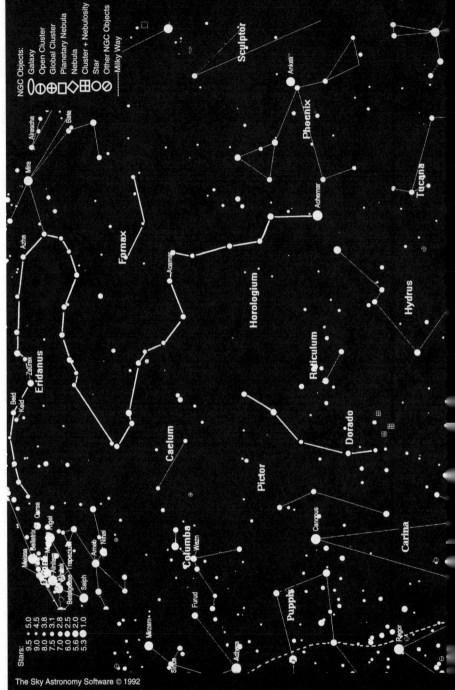

The Sky Astronomy Software © 1992

The horizon is at 12° North Latitude for January 1st..

WINTERTIME SKY LOOKING WEST

The Sky Astronomy Software © 1992

The horizon is at 12° North Latitude for January 1st..

15

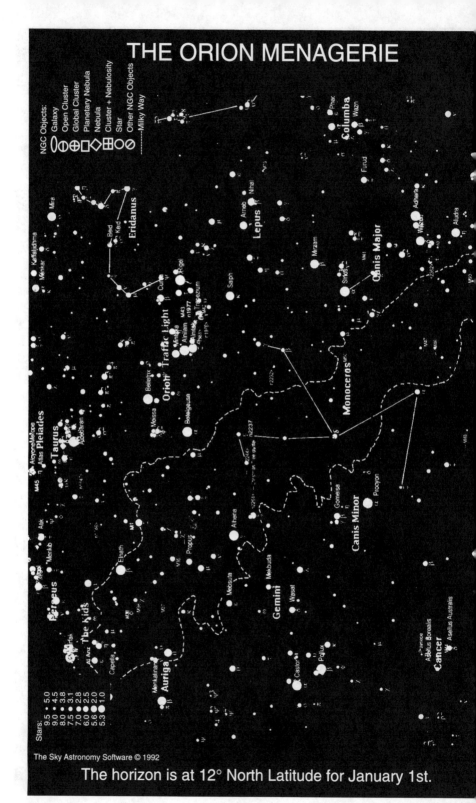

THE ORION MENAGERIE

NGC Objects:
- Galaxy
- Open Cluster
- Global Cluster
- Planetary Nebula
- Nebula
- Cluster + Nebulosity
- Star
- Other NGC Objects
- Milky Way

Stars:
- 9.5 • 5.0
- 9.0 • 4.5
- 8.0 • 3.8
- 7.5 • 3.1
- 7.0 • 2.8
- 6.0 • 2.5
- 5.6 • 2.0
- 5.3 • 1.0

The Sky Astronomy Software © 1992

The horizon is at 12° North Latitude for January 1st.

16

ORION THE GIANT HUNTER

Smack dab in the east on a winter evening is the most distinctive and brightest constellation in the winter sky. If your eye catches three vertical stars in a row, you've got it! This is the belt of Orion the Mighty Warrior or Hunter, the giant of the winter sky.

Orion was a gigantic, handsome hunter and the Greeks believed that he was so tall he could walk through the ocean without wetting his head. Unfortunately, Orion let this all go to his head and boosted to the heavens that he could, if he felt like it, exterminate all the animals of Earth. Gaia, the Goddess of the Earth, happened to hear him and to punish Orion for his arrogance, sent the Scorpion to kill him. When Orion dies and sinks below the western horizon, you may see the claws of Scorpius just rising in the southeast. During the day, Orion is fixed up as good as new by Ophiuchus, the Serpent Bearer, and rises again the next evening. Since then the two enemies, Orion and Scorpius, have been separated and you will never see them in the sky at the same time.

A strange myth about Orion's birth comes from the Greeks. One day the three gods Zeus, Neptune and Hermes, who had just been given a royal feast by Hyrieus, a poor farmer, awarded his generosity by providing a son for him. The three gods stood upon the hide of the cow that they had just consumed, urinated on it and told Hyrieus to bury it. Nine months later a boy was born and the farmer named him Urion after the odd method of his conception. If you look at Orion, who stands upright when he is overhead, you might imagine the whole figure as a cow's hide formed by the four bright stars that bracket Orion's belt.

To the Arabic cultures Orion was a heroic and invincible warrior, kneeling on his right knee with his left foot resting on a footstool. Aloft he holds a sword and a shield or lion's skin in front of him to ward off Taurus the Bull. The Taulipang Indians of northern Brazil also saw a warrior with his foot resting on a footstool made from an animal's head. This is just one of the amazing coincidences of two vastly different peoples, separated by immense distances who envisioned a similar figure.

The ancient Egyptians saw Orion as Osiris, the "God of Light" or the "Moon God." At the Hathor temple of Dendera, Osiris is standing in a celestial boat with his wife Isis and her sister Nephthys. As he sails across the sky, his boat floats on the ocean sky and is supported by four goddesses who represent the four cardinal directions. In the New Kingdom tomb of Senmut, Osiris stands alone in a small canoe, his head turned back to see his wife who is represented by Sirius in Canis Major, the Great Dog. Isis follows Osiris just as Sirius follows Orion across the sky from east to west.

In Egypt Osiris is absent from the night sky for seventy days which is the period Osiris spent in the underworld after he was killed and before he was reborn in the winter. His birth, growth, and death symbolize to the Egyptians and other river people the three seasons of farming and of the Nile — the summer flooding, the emergence of the crop, and the water returned to the soil.

The story of the death of Osiris can be found under Piscis Austrinus, the Southern Fish in the Summertime section. For now, let's examine Orion's Belt which had numerous connotations to many people. The Arabs called it the "Golden Nuts" or "Spangles," but it also reminded them of their white-belted black sheep. Except for the sheep image, the Arabic names of the Belt stars reflect their ideas. The northernmost star, Mintaka (Delta Orionis)[4] is the "Giant's Belt." Alnilam (Epsilon Ori), the middle star, is the "String of Pearls" and Alnitak (Zeta Ori), the southernmost star, the "Girdle." European seamen named the Belt the "Golden Yardarm," while tradesmen referred to it as the "Yardstick." South Americans and Puerto Ricans call it the "Three Kings" or "Three Marias." We could call it the "Traffic Light" because of its resemblance to one which we may use to direct us to other stars and constellations.

* * * * *

The bright orangish star to the north of the Belt is Betelgeuse (Alpha Orionis) whose name in Arabic means "arm-pit of the giant." Betelgeuse is a huge, pulsating, red supergiant and one of the largest stars known. If Betelgeuse was in the same position as the Sun, it would engulf Mercury, Venus, Earth, Mars and possibly extend out to Jupiter. Our eyes cannot detect radiation at all wavelengths, but if they could, Betelgeuse would appear as the brightest star in the sky with a luminosity of 14,000 suns. We see it as the twelfth brightest star. Rigel (Beta Orionis), the seventh brightest star in the sky, is a blazing white-hot supergiant of dazzling beauty. Its computed luminosity is some 57,000 times the brightness of our Sun. If it was as close to us as Sirius, the brightest star in the night sky, it would give us about a fifth the light of a Full Moon.

One of the most extraordinary treasures of the winter sky is M42[5] (NGC-1976)[6], the Orion Nebula[7]. The Orion Nebula is a seething star factory; a caldron of gas and dust 1600 light years away where stars are being born. In binoculars you see a bluish-white, distinctly-shaped glowing fan surrounding Theta Orionis. Embedded in the nebula is a quartet of stars called the Trapezium which, with concentration, can be picked out.

The Orion Nebula is in the center of Orion's dagger that hangs about three degrees or two fingers from his belt to the southeast. If your sky is exceptionally clear, carefully scrutinize the nebula and you may discern M43 (NGC-1982) hovering like a little bright coma on top of it. Keen eyes may also spot NGC-1977, another diffuse nebula above them and crowning these glories is NGC-1981, a bright open cluster. If this is your first experience in picking out star clusters and nebulae, don't get discouraged! Treasure hunting takes practice! Be sure to log the Orion Nebula and its cohorts in your winter treasure chest at the end of the Wintertime section.

The Orionid meteor shower occurs in mid-October. Refer to Appendix III for details.

CANIS MAJOR THE GREAT DOG OR SNOOPY THE SEA DOG

The Chinese saw this Great Dog as the "Celestial Jackal" that steals chickens. To native Australians it is the constellation of the Eagle. Egyptians believed Sirius (Alpha Canis Majoris) was Anubus, a god with a dog's head. Sirius also represented Isis, the wife of Osiris, "the Moon God," whose story is told under Orion.

Sirius may be the most revered star throughout the ages. Its risings and settings were regularly tabulated centuries before the Egyptian pyramids were built. It was immensely important in Egypt because its rising just before the Sun appeared was associated with the overflowing of the Nile. This helical rising heralded the end of the dry, hot summer and the beginning of the fertility of the land. It was believed that the heat of the Sun and that of Sirius caused the very hot weather, which may have led to the term "dog days."

The name Sirius, derived from the Greek *Seirios* means the "Scorcher" or the "Sparkling One." According to the Greeks, people often suffered fevers during the dog days which the doctors called the "Sirius disease." Even dogs were affected and seemed to contract rabies which was known as "lyssa" or "wolfishness." Those possessed with "lyssa" on the battlefield claimed they could "see red."

Thus it's not surprising that Sirius was thought to be a red star and not a brilliant white star. Often it is fiery red and twinkles[8] spectacularly in other colors of the spectrum when it is near the horizon, due to atmospheric scattering. The color red, however, was the most important because it signified disaster. If Sirius rose bright and white, then the Egyptians thought that the Nile would rise high and there would be abundance. If it rose fiery and reddish, there would be war and the weather would be diseased. Perhaps the old adage — "red in the morning, the sailor

Snoopy The Sea Dog (Canis Major)
Dances on the Beach

takes warning, red at night, the sailor delights" — originates from that old superstition.

* * * * *

To find Orion's no. 1 hunting dog, start at Orion's Belt, the Traffic Light, and zip twenty degrees or two handspans held side by side down to Sirius. Sirius, the brilliant blue-white star, represents the head of Snoopy, the top dog around these parts. Look at Snoopy just as Charles Schultz portrayed him in his comic strip "Peanuts." Snoopy dances upright, his right foreleg ending at Mirzam (Beta Canis Majoris). His body forms an upside down elongated "Y" with its base at Wezen (Delta CMa). From Wezen his hind legs are spread wide, the northernmost ending at Aludra (Eta CMa) and the other at Adhara (Epsilon CMa). Just like the shooting stars or dancing coyotes, Snoopy is addicted to dancing, particularly at a jump-up during carnival, but he is still Orion's most faithful hound.

Sirius is a double star, that is, it has a very dense white companion star that orbits it every 50 years. This famous object, called the "Pup," has a density estimated to be some 53,000 times denser than water. A teaspoon of this little star would weigh about 2 1/2 tons per cubic inch on Earth. This amazing dwarf is invisible to the naked eye, yet the Dogon people, who live south of Timbuktu in the Republic of Mali, claim that they have known about it for the last 700 years. Not until 1862 was Sirius B, as it is called, observed in a telescope.

How did the Dogon know about this star? Robert Temple, who wrote "The Sirius Mystery" believes that ancient astronauts from another planet visited Earth and instructed these people. If so, why just them and not the whole world? Perhaps the information didn't come from outer space, but from foreign cultures that integrated with the Dogon. However, this seems unlikely because this belief is indigenous only to the Dogon. What's more, they believe in a third companion orbiting Sirius, a larger and more brilliant star than Sirius. No telescope as yet has found any trace of this mystery star, so the general conclusion is that these stars are symbols of the seasonal agricultural cycle which governed the Dogon people.

One of the most beautiful open star clusters in the winter sky is M41 (NGC-2278) which lies in Snoopy's chest about three fingers or four degrees south of Sirius. It appears as a smudge to the naked eye, but in binoculars is a faint swirl of diamonds. Move down to Wezen (Delta CMa) and enjoy the delicate necklace almost encircling it. NGC-2362, one of the youngest open clusters known, possibly less than one million years, lies about one finger north of the necklace. Notice that the Silver Stream, the Milky Way, courses through Snoopy's body and within it are many intriguing patterns to discover.

CANIS MINOR, THE LITTLE DOG

Standing behind Orion's shoulder is Canis Minor, the Little Dog, with its sparkling star Procyon (Alpha Canis Minoris). To find Procyon draw a line from Orion's shoulder star Betelgeuse (Alpha Orionis) and Melissa (Lambda Ori), his head east to Procyon. Procyon is the eighth brightest star and the fifth closest of the naked eye stars. Procyon means "the dog who rises before Sirius" or just "before the dog." Like Sirius, Procyon has a bright star rising before it bearing the name Mirzam (Beta CMi) which means "announcer." Mirzam is today known by its more popular name, Gomeisa. Similarly, Procyon is a double star and its companion, also a white dwarf, revolves around it about every forty years with a density even greater than that of Sirius' "Pup."

The three stars Sirius, Procyon, and Betelgeuse (Alpha Orionis) form the corners of a huge triangle called the "Winter Triangle." Within this triangle runs the Milky Way Stream and swimming inside it is the almost invisible, fabulous beastie.

MONOCEROS THE CLEVER UNICORN

Separating Orion's two dogs and well hidden, the Unicorn is a challenge to find. It ought to be included under the Obscure Constellations section since none of its stars are brighter than fourth magnitude. Yet, because it has snuck undetected past the two hunting dogs and is almost jabbing Orion in the head with its horn, it should not be overlooked. After all, the Unicorn is doing exactly what it is supposed to do, that is, being a sneaky, but charming creature. Picture if you will, this magical animal with the body and head of a horse, the legs of a deer and the tail of a lion. Cunningly, it stands in the Milky Way Stream where its scent is masked from the Dogs.

The Unicorn was believed to inhabit the Himalaya Mountains of Tibet, one of the most inaccessible and loneliest places on Earth. The Tibetians thought that the new crescent Moon symbolized the Unicorn's horn. The motions of the Sun and the Moon through the sky represented the Unicorn's journeys. The Sun commanded the skies during the day but surrendered them to the Moon, the Unicorn, for the night.

A common belief is that this quiet, mystical animal can only be lured into captivity by the gentleness of a young girl. Another legend says that the horn of a unicorn is magical, rendering poison harmless and protecting anyone who possessed its horn from evil.

* * * * *

Monoceros is found halfway along a line from the Traffic Light to Sirius (Alpha Canis Majoris). Monoceros chose its hiding place well because it is enveloped in complex nebulosity, M50 (NGC-2323). This is a bright, open cluster in binoculars and displays intricate chains of stars. To find M50, sight on a line from Sirius to Procyon (Alpha Canis Minoris). M50 will be about one-third the distance from Sirius and slightly above the line.

A most unusual open star cluster in Monoceros is NGC-2244 found on a line drawn between Betelgeuse (Alpha Orionis) and Procyon. About one-third the distance from Betelgeuse, it looks like a fuzzy star because it is surrounded in a faint haze which is NGC-2237, the famous Rosette Nebula. This nebula encircles the cluster like a doughnut.

Wading up the Stream about five degrees north-north-east from the Rosette Nebula is NGC-2264, the Christmas Tree Cluster, named for its nearly perfect outline of a tree, although some think it is diamond-shaped. Its distinctive pattern is easy to spot and a worthy entry in your treasure chest.

GEMINI THE TWIN SAILORS

Across the Milky Way Stream north of Orion are the Gemini Twins, the warlike heroes and protectors of sailors during violent storms and fighters against pirates. The pair of bright stars, Castor (Alpha Geminorum) and Pollux (Beta Gem) represent the heads of the Twins who lie side by side on a beach, cooling their feet in the Stream. In Greek mythology they helped Jason and the 50 Argonauts recover the golden fleece on a voyage aboard the ship Argo. During lightning storms the Twins sometimes are believed to appear in the ship's rigging in the form of electricity, which leaps from shroud to shroud; a phenomenon called St. Elmo's fire. The exclamation, "By Giminy!" is a modern contraction of an ancient expression of thanks by the sailors to the Twins who saved them.

The outline of the constellation is nearly a perfect rectangle with each long side of the rectangle representing one of the Twins. Sometimes this rectangle is seen as a table at which Castor and Pollux are eating. The two dogs Sirius and Procyon wait patiently for the table crumbs that can be seen as very faint stars scattered between Gemini and Canis Minor.

In the Greek myth Pollux is immortal, but Castor is not. When Castor is killed while trying to prevent cattle from being stolen, Pollux pleads with Jupiter to let him die too. As twins, they are inseparable and cannot live apart. Unfortunately for Pollux, gods don't die, but Pollux is allowed to spend every day with his brother in the underworld. This story is played on the sky screen each evening when Castor rises in the east, closely followed by his brother and when he leaves in the west, Pollux still faithfully follows.

* * * * *

Locate Gemini by curving from Alnilam (Epsilon Orionis), the middle star of the Traffic Light through Betelgeuse (Alpha Ori) to Alhena (Gamma Geminorum) and northeasterly to Pollux (Beta Gem). In binoculars Castor appears as a double star but it actually consists of six stars which revolve around each other. Pollux is yellowish and until the last three centuries was brighter than Castor . The Twins are a rich hunting ground for innumerable star patterns. Strings, loops, twists and other interesting shapes tempt your imagination.

About one finger above Castor's big toe, Propus (Eta Geminorum), is M35 (NGC-2168), a striking open star cluster. In binoculars it is a tangle of chains — or is it a sky rocket? Or a swirl of glittering soap bubbles? Create your own image and stick it in your treasure chest.

Gemini hosts a prolific meteor shower every December. Refer to Appendix III for meteor shower details.

AURIGA THE HERDSMAN

Northeast of Gemini it's a short hop to Auriga, which is depicted today as a pentagon instead of the Persian rendition of a man holding a goat (Capella — Alpha Aurigae) and three kids with one arm, and a bridle and whip

with the other. Auriga also represents the ancient chari-
oteers who looked after the chariots and livestock of their
masters. The constellation is identified with Erichthonius,
a legendary king of Athens who was raised by Athene from
which the name Athens is derived. Erichthonius was the
first man to harness four horses to a chariot, imitating the
Sun Chariot of Helios. Jupiter was so pleased with his
cleverness that he placed Erichthonius among the stars.

Another myth associated with Auriga is about Hippolytus, son of Theseus. In this soap opera Phaedra, his
stepmother, tried to seduce him. When he refused, she
killed herself. For refusing to commit near incest, Hippolytus was banished by Theseus from Athens. As he
raced away in his Corvette, he had a traffic accident and
was killed. Asclepius the healer, also identified with Ophiuchus the Serpent Bearer, took pity on Hippolytus and
brought him back to life. This act made Hades, ruler of the
underworld, furious because he lost more business collect-
ing souls to fry, so the kind but unappreciated Asclepius
was zapped with a thunderbolt by Jupiter. Even on the sky
screen there is no justice!

As a herdsman holding a goat called Amaltheia,
which provided milk for the infant Jupiter on the island of
Crete, Auriga was put in the sky as a gesture of thanks. But
an alternate story relates that Amaltheia was a nymph who
owned the goat. The goat was so wretched that Jupiter
killed it and made a cloak for himself from the goat's hide
and adapted the back of it to look like the head of one of
the Gorgons. It was so frightening to see that it protected
Jupiter from his enemies.

* * * * *

Auriga is located by sighting from Mintaka (Delta
Orionis), the top-most star in the Traffic Light, north
through the horns of Taurus the Bull to bright Capella
(Alpha Aurigae). Capella means "little she-goat" and is the
fifth brightest star. It is the nearest to the North Pole of all
the first-magnitude stars and from the tropics is visible at

some hour of the night throughout most of the year. Capella is a multiple star system and resembles our Sun in age and luminosity.

Close to Capella is a small triangle of three stars called the Kids. The closest star to Capella is Al Anz (Epsilon Aurigae) which is orbited by an enormous, dark, mysterious object that passes in front of it every 27.1 years and cuts off half its light for many months. Astronomers believe it is an immense disk of solid particles seen edge on orbiting around a pair of ordinary stars. If the Sun were put in the center of this disk and the planets Mercury, Venus, Earth, Mars, Jupiter and Saturn were positioned at their correct distances from the Sun, they would all be swallowed up with plenty of room to spare.

Three messy objects, open star clusters, show as bright smudges in binoculars inside and near the pentagon. Find M38 (NGC-1912) halfway and just above a line sighted between Theta and Iota Aurigae. M38 is the dimmest of the three but is almost two-thirds the size of the Full Moon. M36 (NGC 1960) lies only 2.3 degrees southeast of M38 and appears slightly brighter. The last cluster, M37 (NGC-2099) lies just outside and below a line between Theta Aurigae and Al Nath (Gamma Aur). This is the brightest of the lot and in more powerful binoculars may appear more than just a misty glow.

TAURUS THE BLOODSHOT-EYED BULL

Taurus the Bull lies west of Orion and below Auriga. The tip of the left horn, Elnath (Beta Tauri), the "Butting One" is shared with Auriga, where it is Gamma Aurigae. Taurus rises upside down and backwards with only his head and shoulders visible. What happened to the rest of the beast? Perhaps when the Sumerians invented it before 3500 B.C., Taurus had a full body, but now Cetus the Whale and Eridanus the River have replaced it.

Taurus was not only a powerful and strong bull, but also a good, kind beast. Two conflicting Roman legends involve the Bull. One relates that Jupiter fell in love with Europa and decided to carry her off — literally. Being a god, he could change himself into anything, so Jupiter became a beautiful white bull, so friendly and attentive to Europa that she climbed upon his back for a ride. Aha! He took her and galloped off with his prize.

The other tale has Europa as Io, a lovely priestess, with whom Jupiter becomes involved. Juno, Jupiter's wife, found out about the affair and changes Io into a white heifer and had her kept prisoner by the giant Argus with one hundred eyes. Eventually Jupiter had her rescued and placed her in the sky so that Io would be safe from Juno. So, depending upon which legend you prefer, the Bull could really be a cow.

To find Taurus, slightly curve a line from Mintaka (Delta Orionis), the top star in the Traffic Light, up to bright, orangish Aldebaran (Alpha Tauri). The brightest eye-catcher in Taurus is its bloodshot eye Aldebaran from the Arabic, meaning the "Follower of the Pleiades." Ptolemy in his *Tetrabiblos* called it the "Torch," presumably because of its color. This reddish gleaming star that resembles Betelgeuse (Alpha Orionis) forms the left eye of the V-shaped forehead of Taurus. When you locate this V, which lies slightly sideways and upside down, you may see the group of double stars within the V gleaming like little twin bees. These are the double stars called the Hyades who are the half sisters of the Pleaides. The Hyades are known as the "Rain-Bringing Stars" because they wept so copiously after their Earth-bound brother Hyas had drowned in a well, that their tears caused torrential rainfall. The Hyades cluster is gravitationally bound, but Aldebaran, the cool, obese supergiant beside them does not belong to the group. The Hyades are about twice as far from Earth as Aldebaran and are moving eastward toward Betelgeuse.

Lying about one degree west of Zeta Tauri is M1 (NGC-1952), the famous Crab Nebula, named by the astronomer Lord Rosse because of its resemblance to a crab. Although you can't see it without a telescope, its importance must be noted. The Crab Nebula looks like a misty patch, the remnant of a supernova which exploded in A.D. 1054. When the Chinese who recorded it saw it appear abruptly one night, the explosion of the star had already occurred 4000 years previously. The nebula is still expanding at approximately 70 million miles per day.

Two open star clusters in the horns of Taurus are worth a visit. NGC-1647 is about a fourth of the distance on a line drawn from Aldebaran (Alpha Tauri) to Zeta, the tip of the eastern or lower horn. It is a faint, misty glow duplicated by NGC-1746, the other open cluster about half way down the line to Zeta.

M45, the Pleiades star cluster, in the shoulder of Taurus is explored in the next chapter.

The Taurid meteor shower occurs every October. Refer to Appendix III for details.

The Pleiades Star Cluster

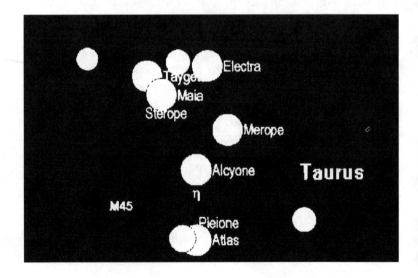

The Seven Indian Maidens Escape From the Bear at Devil's Tower

THE PLEIADES,
THE SEVEN SISTERS CLUSTER

Pinned to the Bull's hump is the diamond brooch, M45, the Pleiades. Its seven brightest stars are the Seven Sisters, the daughters of Atlas and Pleione. The stars are also seen as a flock of birds. In one story the Sisters were sometimes pursued by Orion, an overeager suitor. Venus changed the frightened girls into a flock of doves so that they could flutter away to safety.

In one native American story the Pleiades were seven children who liked to hike in the sky. The stars were so numerous that they became lost and couldn't find their way home. They huddled close together so that they wouldn't become separated. After a spell they got homesick and wept for their family on Earth. Their tears represent the nebulosity in which the stars are enmeshed, making them appear somewhat bleary-eyed.

Another native American legend involves the Devil's Tower, an impressive rock formation rising abruptly 1300 feet above the plains of northeastern Wyoming. This tower was raised up by the Great Spirit to protect seven Indian maidens who were pursued by a giant bear. Later they were placed in the sky as the Pleiades cluster and the marks of the bear's claws may be seen on the sides of the Tower as vertical striations.

Rising in the east, high above Orion, the Pleiades are a tiny but conspicuous cluster. As seasonal heralds, their risings and settings have been used extensively to regulate calendars, festivals and rituals and to influence or coincide with changes in the weather.

It is no wonder that this glistening strand of diamonds has set the imaginations of countless poets on fire. How beautifully they are described by Lord Alfred Tennyson in his *Locksley Hall:*

"Many a night I saw the Pleiades, rising through the
mellow shade,
Glitter like a swarm of fire-flies tangled in a silver
braid."

* * * * *

The Pleiades may have been the first stars mentioned
in astronomical literature, appearing in Chinese annals of
2357 B.C. Their name may be derived from the Greek word
plien meaning "to sail" or possibly from the Greek *pe-
leiades*, meaning "flock of doves."

At one time one of the sisters, Electra (17 Tauri) or
Merope (23 Tauri), was "lost" because people could see
only six stars. Electra and Merope are variable stars and in
legends become dim because their tears mask their beauty.
Merope is particularly surrounded by reflection nebulosity, very faint dust which shines by reflected starlight from
the other sisters. This delicate light has been said to resemble "breath on a mirror."

The Pleiades cluster ranks as one of the most beautiful
gems in your treasure chest. With your naked eye you may
see up to eight or nine stars on a clear night, although most
people can only pick out six. With binoculars, more than
one hundred may be visible. Look for the two delicate
threads of tiny stars which loop through the cluster from
the north and south.

LEPUS THE HARE OR EASTER BUNNY

Lepus the Hare crouches silently below Orion's feet,
his ears west of Rigel (Beta Orionis), the bright blue-white
foot of Orion. Lepus is not a dumb bunny, for he knows
that if he moves, he will be detected by Orion's hunting
dogs, Sirius (Alpha Canis Majoris) and Procyon (Alpha
Canis Minoris).

At one time Lepus had been a bird, but fortunately he did not retain his bird brain. Ostara, the Goddess of Spring whose name, meaning Easter, is derived from the German word *Ostern*, changed him into a hare. Once a year he is allowed to lay eggs like the bird he once was. Today he is the Easter Bunny and carries the eggs on his back.

* * * * *

Lepus is a dim constellation compared to Orion, but it has a noticeable lopsided square of stars which can be seen as his head or his body. Two bright stars above the square represent the tips of his ears. Lepus may be located from Alnilam (Epsilon Orionis), the middle star in the Traffic Light, by drawing a line down through Orion's dagger that points right at Lepus.

Lepus contains one globular star cluster, M79 (NGC-1904), visible in binoculars on a clear, dark night. Look on a line from Arneb (Alpha Leporis) through Nihal (Beta Lep) and extend it a little farther than the distance between these two stars.

Close to the hind legs of the Hare is Gamma Leporis, a double star of yellow and greenish hues.

ERIDANUS THE RIVER

Eridanus is the river in which Phaethon, the son of Helios, drowns after being catapulted out of the Sun Chariot during his wild, destructive ride across the sky. The River has been associated with the major rivers of many nations such as the Nile, the Euphrates, the Po, the Rhine, the Rhone and the Yellow River of China.

The Arabian and other nomadic people had a completely different idea, identifying Eridanus as two ostriches with chicks in their two nests, complete with eggs and broken egg shells. Each nest, containing one or two chicks, is snuggled under the first two bends of the River, followed by the two ostriches who are standing in the water.

* * * * *

Eridanus is like a roller coaster, meandering up and down across the southeastern sky. It is the longest constellation and although most of its stars are faint, it is not hard to trace. Close to bright Rigel (Beta Orionis), Orion's foot is Cursa (Beta Eridani) where the River begins. Cursa means the "chair" or "footstool of the Central One," on which Orion supported his left foot. From Cursa, the River begins its first giant arch that plummets to Theemin (Tau9 Eridani) and Beemin (Tau8 Eri), a duo of stars. Rising northward it heads for Acamar (Theta Eri) and finally plunges down to end at the ninth brightest star, Achernar (Alpha Eri), the most prominent star in the south next to Canopus (Alpha Carinae) in Carina the Keel. Originally the name Achernar, meaning the "End of the River," was given to the star now called Acamar (Theta Eri) because it terminated the River at the latitude of the Mediterranean. After the European seafarers sailed further south, their imaginations projected the River down to Achernar.

* * * * *

Achernar (Alpha Eridani) is a brilliant, bluish star in the south rivaled only by Canopus (Alpha Carinae). It is unmistakable as it stands alone in an area of dim stars. There is no other star with which it can be confused except for Canopus that rises well to the east.

THE WINTER SECTION OF ARGO THE SAILING SHIP

The horizon is at 12° North Latitude for March 1st.

CARINA THE KEEL AND VELA THE SAIL

Argo Navis was the largest of the first 48 constellations catalogued by Ptolemy in A.D. 150. In 1763 the French astronomer Nicolas Louis de Lacaille divided the large, unwieldy constellation into three sections: Carina the Keel, Vela the Sail and Puppis the Stern. At one time there was also Malus the Mast, but it somehow got lost in the shuffle. Another constellation, Pyxis the Ship's Compass, was curiously placed near what used to be the masthead. The ship now has no bow and nothing but air to support the sail. The Milky Way Stream courses through the Ship, creating a confusion of stars and making it one of the best starfields the southern sky has to offer.

The ship Argo, the "Swift One," was built for Jason to search for and return the Golden Fleece from the Ram to his country. Among his crew were the Twins (Castor and Pollux), Hercules, Orpheus (the singer with the magical voice), Theseus, (the hero who slew the Minotaur), and many others. Jason and his men had many adventures, one of which is related under Columba the Winter Bird. When they found the Golden Fleece, which was guarded by an immortal dragon, they knew it was impossible to kill it. The dragon had to be tricked into giving the Golden Fleece to them and that would be no easy task. The dragon, however, had a passion for chocolate, so Jason gave him a milk shake that had a sleeping draught in it. The dragon eagerly slurped it down and fell asleep, allowing Jason to remove the fleece and begin their journey home.

* * * * *

Argo rises stern first so that the eye is immediately drawn to Canopus (Alpha Carinae) that represents the rudder. Canopus is the second brightest star in the night sky and is thought to be at least 60,000 times more luminous than the Sun. Canopus is named after the chief pilot of the Greek King Menelaus. Egyptians knew it as the "Golden Earth" and like other desert people worshipped the star, building temples to it so that at the time of the autumnal equinox in 6400 B.C., it heralded the sunrise. The Arabs called Canopus "Suhail", a name applied to persons of exceptional beauty and brilliance. Canopus was generally considered to be the southern pole star and was a primary navigational aid.

Begin your exploration of Carina and Vela by star-hopping from the Traffic Light down to Sirius (Alpha Canis Majoris) and straight south across to brilliant Canopus (Alpha Carinae). At Canopus zip eastward two handspans to the brightest of the stars in that area, Regor (Gamma Velorum) in Vela. It is a stunning multiple star of white, green and purple colors, aptly named the "Spectral Gem" of the southern skies.

Treasure chest material abounds south of Regor (Gamma Velorum). Only two degrees or one fat finger south of Regor is NGC-2547, an outstanding star cluster with many twists and swirls. Six degrees or three fingers southeast of this cluster and northwest about one finger above bright Delta Carinae is IC 2391, the brightest cluster in the constellation. IC 2395, another but small cluster is about 6° or a fist north of IC 2391. After this exciting sightsee, put aside your binoculars and look for Carina's famous asterism, the False Cross. The False Cross rises on its side and is formed by Delta Velorum and Markab (Kappa Vel), and Iota Carinae and Avior (Epsilon Car) at the foot. A couple of fingers west of Avior and 15° southeast of Canopus (Alpha Carinae) is the stunning bright conglomerate NGC-2516, easily visible to the naked eye as a dappled smudge, but in binoculars is a sparkling brooch. Further attractions in Carina become visible in the spring and are explored in the Springtime section of the southern sky.

* * * * *

PUPPIS THE STERN

Forming the high poop deck of the fifteenth-century square-rigged vessels, Puppis rears in Argo Navis above Carina the Keel. It is adjacent to Canis Major and abuts Monoceros. The Milky Way Stream flows right through Puppis and contains three messy objects which jut out as if they were isolated, misty islands.

* * * * *

Starting at the Traffic Light, shoot two handspans down to Sirius (Alpha Canis Majoris). About fifteen degrees or one and a half handspans east and a little north of Sirius is the first of the messy objects, M46 (NGC-2437), a bright knot of stars. In the same field pick up M47 (NGC-2422), another cluster slightly brighter. To find the third cluster, head down from Sirius to Wezen (Delta Canis Majoris) that marks the base of Snoopy's body. M93 (NGC-2447) is about four fingers below Wezen.

Two outstanding clusters in Puppis are in its lower section, NGC-2451 and NGC-2477. To find them take a line from Sirius (Alpha CMa) through Wezen (Delta CMa) down some fifteen degrees until you intersect these sparkling beehives. NGC-2451, the larger and brighter of the two, may remind you of a silver bowl filled with M & Ms. Its cohort, NGC-2477, is a bright speckled ball about the size of the Full Moon.

PYXIS THE SHIP'S COMPASS

Pyxis the Ship's Compass was invented by de Lacaille when he divided Argo. It floats above Vela the Sail where Malus the Mast once was. The arrangement is peculiar and it is unlikely that there was a compass aboard Argo.

* * * * *

Pyxis has only three stars of fourth magnitude that are just discernible to the eye. They represent the steel needle in early compasses that was wiped with a lodestone to give it its magnetic properties. The needle, fastened to a small piece of wood, floated in a bowl of water and indicated north. Pyxis borders the upper section of Puppis to its east and seems to point across the Milky Way Stream northward to Alphard (Alpha Hydrae), the brightest star in Hydra, the Female Water Snake.

COLUMBA THE WINTER BIRD

Columba the Dove is sometimes referred to as Columba Noae, Noah's Dove, which was sent out by Noah to see if the waters had receded and land had appeared. The dove returned, bearing an olive branch and Noah realized that the trees were reappearing and dry land would surface soon. When he again released the dove and it did not return, Noah knew that it had at last found land.

Columba is also associated with the ship on its voyage with Jason and the Argonauts who were searching for the golden fleece. One day Argo was approaching the dreaded rocks of the Symplegades that guard the passage between the Aegean and Black Seas. These treacherous rocks would crash together from either side, crushing anything attempting to pass through. Jason knew of this danger and sent the brave little bird to fly swiftly through the rocks to determine if there was any chance the ship could be rowed through without being crushed. An instant after Columba sped through, the rocks smashed together — WHAM! — and nipped off a few tail feathers. A close call! This incident may be the reason why there are no long tail feathers pictured on the dove and no stars that mark the tail. Jason was able to row through safely enough, although the ship was damaged at the stern. Since then, the rocks have remained still and the dove was rewarded for its bravery by being given snow-white plumage and placed in the sky.

To find Columba take a line from Alnilam (Epsilon Orionis) the middle star of the Traffic Light, and follow it through Orion's dagger to Arneb (Alpha Leporis) in Lepus to Phact (Alpha Columbae). A small sprinkle of stars, eight of them easily visible to the naked eye, form the dove. A fainter sprinkle of stars that may represent the remains of Columba's tail is shown better in binoculars.

One globular star cluster, NGC-1851, is visible in binoculars as a faint little blob in Columba's southwestern corner and may be found if a line is extended from Mu Columbae through Phact (Alpha Col) and Epsilon about three fingers to the cluster.

Whoops! Columba the Dove Loses Its Tail Feathers Between the Symplegades

VI

The Winter Obscure Constellations

*F*ive constellations placed near the lower bends of Eridanus the River were created by the French astronomer, the Abbe Nicolas Louis de Lacaille in the mid-eighteenth century and have no ancient legends connected to them. Fornax the Furnace is composed of the faint stars that are bracketed by the bends of the River on the northwest side. Caelum the Burin is sandwiched below the first dip of the River above Columba. West of Caelum is Horologium, the Pendulum Clock, lying sideways and stretching from Caelum almost to Achernar (Alpha Eridani), the "End of the River." Below Caelum and above Canopus (Alpha Carinae) is Pictor the Painter's Easel. Below Horologium is Reticulum which represented a reticle but is today called the Net. None of these constellations have stars brighter than fourth magnitude and are best seen in a dark sky.

Thrust between Pictor and Reticulum is Dorado the Gold Fish or Dolphin that Johannes Bayer included in his charts in 1603. To find Dorado start at Canopus (Alpha Carinae) and move south-southwest twelve degrees to a trapezoid of stars that contain Beta, Delta and G Doradus. Four degrees south of this trapezoid is the glowing Large Magellanic Cloud (LMC). The Dorado is plunging toward the South Pole, his tail and body drawn along a line of stars. Dorado appears to be chomping on the Large Magellanic Cloud (LMC), a satellite galaxy that orbits our Milky Way Galaxy. The expedition commanded by Ferdinand Magellan, the Portuguese navigator in the early sixteenth century, was probably responsible for creating Dorado along with its neighbor Volans, the Flying Fish.

* * * * *

Dorado leaps above and to the west of Canopus (Alpha Carinae) with only the faint stars of Pictor between them. The stars of Dorado are dim and hard to trace southward, but there is no mistaking the LMC which appears like a huge, glowing misty patch. It is an arresting sight, the undisputed glory of the southern winter sky. About 170,000 light years away, the LMC contains NGC-2070, the extraordinary Tarantula or Great Looped Nebula. It is one of the largest emission nebulae known and if it were as close to us as the Orion Nebula, it would cover 30 degrees of the sky. NGC-2070 contains S-Doradus, the most luminous star yet discovered. In the LMC Supernova 1987A, a huge star, suddenly exploded and thrilled astronomers worldwide in 1987 because it was the first supernova to be observed in telescopes in nearly four hundred years.

Next to the LMC is Mensa the Table which de Lacaille created as a tribute to the renowned 4,000-foot high mesa-like Table Mountain rising above Capetown, South Africa. Perhaps de Lacaille placed Mensa under the LMC because its mistiness symbolized the Tablecloth, a large cloud that frequently caps Table Mountain.

YOUR WINTER TREASURE CHEST

| DATE | TIME | LOCATION | WEATHER | | | OBJECT NAME |
| | | | Clouds? | Haze? | Moon Phase | And No. |

YOUR WINTER TREASURE CHEST

Constellation	Type of Object Clus, Gal, Neb	Binocs/eye (Type)	Description Shape, Color Brightness	Comments

Spring Sky Preview

Striding unchallenged across the Springtime sky in the east is the King of the Beasts, Leo the Lion. The Bears in the north are pursued by the three hunters while Hydra the Female Water Snake slithers toward the southeast, the naughty Crow and the Beaker balanced on its back. M44, the Beehive Cluster in Cancer the Crab bristles with bees and the delicate tresses of Coma Berenices are sprinkled with pearls.

The southern sky unfolds more treasures, revealing the rest of Carina the Keel in Argo the Ship, the wise Centaur and the timepiece of the south, Crux the Southern Cross with its Coal Sack and Jewel Box. Nearby the Eta Carinae Nebula and accompanying escorts astound the eye and Omega Centauri in Centaurus, the most dazzling and largest of all globular star clusters, stands out as a giant powder puff. With all these wondrous attractions, the spring sky screen has outdone itself!

SPRINGTIME SKY LOOKING NORTH

NGC Objects:
- Galaxy
- Open Cluster
- Global Cluster
- Planetary Nebula
- Nebula
- Cluster + Nebulosity
- Star
- Other NGC Objects
- Milky Way

Stars:
- 9.5 : 5.0
- 9.0 : 4.5
- 8.0 : 3.8
- 7.5 : 3.1
- 7.0 : 2.8
- 6.0 : 2.5
- 5.6 : 2.0
- 5.3 : 1.0

Canes Venatici

Cor Cai
Chara
Akaid
Edasich
Mizar
Alcor
Alioth
Thuban
Megrez
Phecda
Kochab
Pherkad
Leo Minor
Che
Zosma
Alula Australis
Alula Borea
Tania Australis
Tania Borealis
Ursa Major
Merak
Dubhe
Giausar
Ursa Minor
Talitha
Muscida
Polaris
Lynx
Cameloparmdus
Errai
Pollux
Castor
ni
Auriga
Menkalinan
Capella
Mirfak

The Sky Astronomy Software © 1992

The horizon is at 12° North Latitude for April 1st.

47

SPRINGTIME SKY LOOKING EAST

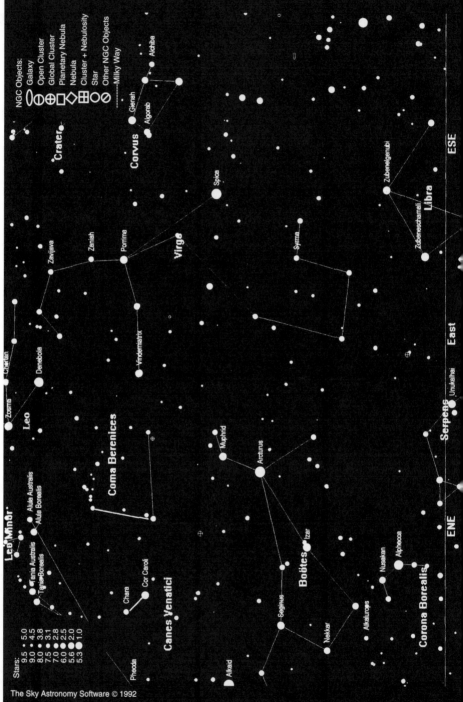

The Sky Astronomy Software © 1992

The horizon is at 12° North Latitude for April 1st.

48

SPRINGTIME SKY LOOKING SOUTH

The horizon is at 12° North Latitude for April 1st.

The Sky Astronomy Software © 1992

SPRINGTIME SKY LOOKING WEST

The Sky Astronomy Software © 1992

The horizon is at 12° North Latitude for April 1st.

THE BEARS AND COMPANIONS

The horizon is at 12° North Latitude for March 1st.

The Sky Astronomy Software © 1992

URSA MAJOR THE GREAT BEAR AND THE BIG DIPPER ASTERISM

The most well-known constellation in the sky is Ursa Major, the Great Bear. Although most people only recognize its famous asterism, the "Big Dipper," the Bear fills a large part of the northern sky with its body and three of its legs. Its counterpart, Ursa Minor, the Little Bear, circles beside it, tying the two together in many legends.

The classic Greek story tells us that Callisto, a beautiful princess of Arcadia, was hunting in the forest when she was accosted by Jupiter in disguise and seduced by him. Outcast because of her resulting pregnancy she remained in the forest and bore a little boy named Arcas. Juno, Jupiter's queen, found out about Callisto and her baby and in a rage changed Callisto into a bear. Many years later Callisto came suddenly upon Arcas, now a grown handsome hunter, and ran to embrace him, forgetting that she was a bear. Arcas prepared to shoot her, but Jupiter saw her plight and to save her, turned Arcas into a bear. Grasping their stubby tails, he flung them with great force into the sky and stretched their tails, making them rather unique-looking.

Consequently, Juno became insanely jealous because Callisto was the brilliant new star goddess for the whole world to see. Juno appealed to the gods to at least prevent Callisto and Arcas from ever bathing in the ocean. Their paws never touch the water except in the lower latitudes, such as in the Caribbean.

A story that parallels the Callisto myth comes from the Iroquois and the Mirmac Indians of northeastern America. The hunt began in the spring when the Bear (with its normal short tail) appeared from her den that was thought to be Corona Borealis, the Northern Crown, a circlet of stars below Boötes the Bear Keeper. The Bear was pursued by seven hunters, but by midsummer only three were left; Robin, Chickadee and Moose Bird. Around autumn the Bear stood erect, ready to confront the hunters. She was killed by Robin and her blood stained his breast, which is how the Robin got its red breast. The autumn leaves, upon which the Bear had fallen, also turn red, which explains the change of colors. Chickadee and Robin cut up the Bear and cooked it in their little pot represented by Alcor (Zeta Ursae Majoris). Moose Bird, being lazy, had hung back to let the others finish the work and then arrived for his share. His name means "He Who Comes In at the Last Moment." During the winter the skeleton of the Bear remains on its back, but by spring the spirit of the Bear has returned and she reappears from her den.

An amusing variation of the hunt story is about the bear who was chased, not by hunters, but by an oak tree. The trees in this particular forest danced after midnight. The bear, wandering through the forest, inadvertently collided with an oak tree. The injured tree, angry because the bear did not apologize, threw it into the heavens by its tail.

Different figures other than the "Big Dipper" are seen in other parts of the world. The British refer to the "Big Dipper" as the "Plough," while the Northern Europeans imagine a great "Wagon and Three Horsemen." A stretcher or litter was seen by a variety of people such as the Arabs, North Africans and central North Americans. The Egyptians had elaborate imaginations as they pictured the Dipper as the "Hind Leg of a Bull."

* * * * *

All the stars of the "Big Dipper" are approaching our system at various speeds. It has been computed from their proper motions that they will form a spread out steamer chair 50,000 years from now. fifty thousand years ago they formed a splendid cross.

The Arabic names and meanings of the four stars comprising the pan of the "Big Dipper" are Dubhe (Alpha Ursae Majoris), the "Back" and Merak (Beta UMa), the "Groin", the pointer stars, Phecda (Gamma UMa), the "Thigh" and Megrez (Delta), the "Root of the Tail." In the handle are Alioth (Epsilon) the "Fat Tail," Mizar (Zeta) the

The Great Bear (Ursa Major) is Chased by Robin, Chicadee and Moose Bird

"Girdle" or "Waist-Cloth," with Alcor, a line of sight star and Alkaid or Benetnasch (Eta), the "Chief of the Mourners."

The origin of Alcor and of Alioth (Epsilon) may have been identical but Alcor in recent times was called the "Test" and the "Faint One." Being able to see Alcor was considered to be a test of one's eyesight when Alcor may have been dimmer than it is today. In Europe, Alcor was the "Little Starry Horseman", a similar idea to the British identity of Mizar (Zeta) as the "Horse" and Alcor as "Jack, the Rider." Mizar and Alcor are gravitationally bound and each has a companion star too faint to be seen without a telescope.

In the Teutonic lands Alcor was Hans the Thumpkins, a wagoner who, in one version, gave Christ a lift and as a reward was elevated to the wagon driver of the Heavenly Wagon. Another Teutonic tale relates that their giant, Orwandil, who is the same as Orion the Hunter, froze one of his big toes. The god Thor snapped it off and threw it at the middle horse pulling the wagon.

Ursa Major hosts at least three bright galaxies within binocular range. On a line extended from Phecda (Gamma UMa) through Dubhe (Alpha) to the northwest about an equal distance is M81 (NGC-3031) a spiral galaxy and M82 (NGC-3034). M101 (NGC-5457), the Pinwheel Galaxy, forms a perfect equal triangle with Mizar (Zeta) and Alioth (Eta). A steady hand is needed to pick out this large but obscure galaxy.

URSA MINOR THE LITTLE BEAR AND POLARIS THE NORTH STAR

Following the Callisto myth that was told under Ursa Major, Arcas, Callisto's son by Jupiter, is Ursa Minor the Little Bear. The Little Bear has been drawn in two different ways, one with its back to Ursa Major and the other with its feet pointed towards her. The Little Bear was recognized as a constellation around 600 B.C. when it began to be used as the chief navigational aid in place of the Greater Bear.

The Arabs saw the constellation as the "Fish" or the "Hole" in which the axle of the sky revolved. On the Nile it was known as the "Jackal" and sometimes the "Hippopotamus" or "Crocodile." Among the northern nations of Europe it was the "Little Wagon" except for the Finns who perceived it as the "Smaller Bear."

Since Sumerian times the constellation was identified with the "Holy Mountain" on which it was believed heaven rested.

Norsemen had the same idea and called it the "Hill of Heaven." This belief in a mythical mountain was carried down to the time of Christopher Columbus who referred to it as "Paria" upon which the "Earth, not being perfectly rounded rested thereon."

"Phoenice" was the early Greek name for the North Star as well as "Stella Polaris," the "Pole Star" and now "Polaris." English seafarers saw it as the "Steering Star" which became the "Lodestar," the leading star. It was the "Star of the North" to Arabia and it was believed that gazing upon it would cure the common desert ailment of itching eyelids.

The charming title of the "Star That Does Not Walk Around" given to the North Star by the Pawnee of central Nebraska clearly defines its uniqueness. They believed that the star patterns around the North Star formed the "Little Stretcher," which carried a sick child. The "Large Stretcher" was the "Big Dipper," which formed four stretcher bearers followed by "Medicine Man," his wife and "Errand Man." Throughout their journeys the "Star That Does Not Walk Around" carefully guarded them.

The Chumash tribes of southern California called the North Star the "Star That Never Moves." This star separated the sky into two sections from north to south. The first half of the day the Sun was in the eastern section and in the second half it was in the western. To the Omahas it represented the center of the four directions and was the imaginary axis of the Earth. North Americans today know it as the end of the "Little Dipper."

* * * * *

Contrary to popular belief, Polaris is not a bright star, being only about magnitude two and a half. What is important about Polaris is that it is just one degree and fourteen minutes from the true north. In the year 2095 it will reach its closest position to the North Pole. It will not return to that position until about 25,700 years later. Surplanting it will be various stars in Cepheus, Cygnus, in Lyra, Hercules and Draco, but there will be periods involving thousands of years when there will not be any north star because there will be none close enough to true north to earn that name.

The easiest way to find Polaris is to take a line from Merek (Beta Ursae Majoris) and Dubhe, (Alpha UMa) the pointer stars in the pan of the "Big Dipper," which point straight to it. Marking the end of Ursa Minor are Kochab (Beta UMi) and Pherkad (Gamma UMi), known as the "Regimen of the North." Imagine the North Star as the center of a clock, with Kochab (Beta) and Pherkad (Gamma) from the hour hand revolving counter-clockwise around it at fifteen degrees an hour. In a twelve-hour night this hour hand revolves 180 degrees. Mariners knew approximately how much time had passed after determining the positions of Kochab and Pherkad each evening from astronomical tables.

If you were to divide this clock into four segments of forty-five degrees each and kept a log of the positions of the hour hand from night to night, you might get a pretty good idea of the time. Put away your wristwatch and test your ability. Don't cheat!

The Ursid meteor shower occurs just before Christmas. Refer to Appendix III for details.

BOÖTES THE BEAR KEEPER AND CANES VENATICI HIS HUNTING DOGS

Boötes, which means "Ox Driver", is the Bear Keeper or Bear Driver who follows the Bears around Polaris. He is also known as the Herdsman or Ploughman because he was credited with the invention of the plough to make the tilling of the Earth easier for all people. As a reward for his generosity, Boötes was placed prominently in the sky.

A tragic classical story about Boötes as Icarius, a grape grower, told of his being befriended by a disguised Bacchus, the God of Wine, who showed him how to make wine. The results delighted Icarius who gave a big party for his pals who became drunk and fell asleep. As they gradually awoke, his friends decided that Icarius had really tried to poison them and they killed him while he slept and threw him into a deep crevasse. His hunting dogs, Asterion and Chara, sensed his death and began to whine so alarmingly that Erigone, the daughter of Icarius, released them from their kennel. The dogs found Icarius's body and Erigone, completely overcome by grief, killed herself by jumping into the ditch. The dogs followed Erigone and died beside their master.

Asterion is formed by two stars, the brightest called Cor Caroli (Alpha Canum Venaticorum), the "Heart of Cor Caroli," named by Sir Edmund Halley for Charles II.

Boötes is kite-shaped but a modern imagination may see it as a chocolate ice cream cone upside down and slightly canted, with Arcturus (Alpha Boötis), the bright orangish star, forming the tip. To find Boötes extend the arc of the handle of the Big Dipper to Arcturus. Arcturus, the fourth brightest star, glows like a hot coal and has no competition with any other bright star in the vicinity. Its rich golden-orange hue was admired from the earliest eras. To the Chinese, Arcturus was the "Great Horn." To the Arabs, it was the "Lofty Lance-bearer." Arcturus was possibly the first star on record to be observed in the daytime with the telescope. It is famous for opening the World Fair in Chicago in 1933 when its light was focused on a photo-electric cell and generated a current that illuminated the Fair.

CORONA BOREALIS
THE NORTHERN CROWN

Corona Borealis, an exquisite circlet with its opening to the north, is southeast of Boötes the Bear Keeper. It was thought to be the Great Bear's den in the native American Bear Hunt. From the southwest comes a charming love story of native American lore.

Algon, a young chieftain, was toolin' along on his Harley Davison through the hills when he saw, in a distant clearing, a circle of star princesses singing and dancing. Each had long glistening hair entwined with stars and their silver dresses and slippers were speckled with stars. Algon hid his bike and crept to the edge of the clearing where he hid and watched the girls.

The next night Algon returned to the clearing early to hide as close as possible before the star princesses returned. Poof! Quicker than a wink they appeared, formed a circle, and danced all night long. Algon fell in love with Ariadne, the prettiest one of them all. Deciding that he couldn't let Ariadne go back to the sky, he changed himself into a mouse and scurried out to the girls. The star princesses were not frightened of mice and they were enchanted with the little creature. When Ariadne picked up the mouse, Algon changed himself quickly back into his human form and grabbed Ariadne. Quickly he zoomed away with her on his bike back to his village and they fell in love and became man and wife.

Look at the Northern Crown and notice that a star is missing in the opening. That is the place where Ariadne used to dance. Her star sisters have left it open for her in case she ever decides to return.

In the Greek legend the Northern Crown is the golden tiara that Bacchus, the God of Wine, placed in the sky to show mankind and all the gods that Ariadne, the daughter of Minos, King of the island of Crete, was the most beautiful of all mortal women. Ariadne consented to marry Bacchus, received immortality and is represented by the brightest and most beautiful stars in the Crown. Gemma, the Gem Star, is also called Alphecca (Alpha Coronae Borealis).

* * * * *

The Northern Crown is a distinctive and pretty circlet of stars a bit over a handspan below Arcturus. The open part of the circle faces the north. The Arabians and other desert peoples called the Crown the "Bright Dish" and the "Beggar's Bowl." Siberians saw it as the "Boot of Kilu" and the "Polar Bear's Paw" while Pacific islanders saw a sting ray or a fishnet. Most imaginative of all were the Chinese who saw Koan-so, the "Money String" made with coins having holes through which the string was threaded.

Algon Watches the Dancing Star Princess (Corona Borealis)

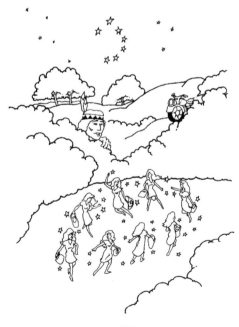

THE VIRGIN AND HER PLAYMATES

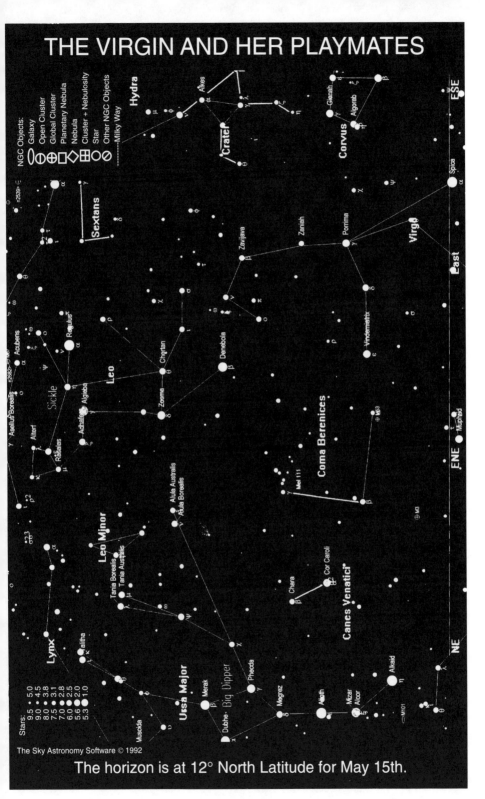

The Sky Astronomy Software © 1992

The horizon is at 12° North Latitude for May 15th.

VIRGO THE VIRGIN

Virgo the Virgin reclines in the southeastern sky clutching a tube of suntan lotion beside her hip. This description may sound farfetched except when one learns of the Oriental description of a sunburnt damsel brandishing an ear of corn. The constellation is very old and has mostly been associated with agriculture and justice. Sometimes Virgo is shown holding a sheaf of wheat as the Goddess of the Harvest.

In Roman times Virgo was identified with Proserpina, the daughter of Ceres, the Goddess of the Fields and Growing Crops. Proserpina was abducted by Pluto to his Underworld. Ceres was so grief-stricken by the loss of Proserpina that she refused to help the crops grow. A famine was imminent until Jupiter intervened. He specified that Proserpina be allowed to live with Pluto six months of the year; the other six she would be with her mother in the Upperworld. This is the reason why we see Virgo from spring to fall when the grain and other crops are grown and harvested. The rest of the year when she is with Pluto, nothing grows because Proserpina's mother misses her so much that she neglects the fields.

As the Goddess of Justice, Virgo is depicted as Astrea holding scales and a sword. In modern times these scales were transferred to Libra, the twelfth zodiacal constellation, which was originally the claws belonging to Scorpius. Virgo was also Erigone, the daughter of Icarius or Boötes who was so ruthlessly murdered and pitched into a crevice. Erigone, along with Boötes and his Hunting Dogs (Canes Venatici) was transported to the heavens.

In Egypt, Virgo was Isis who was threatened by the monster Typhon. She ran away so fast that she dropped a sheaf of grain which spread all over the road. The Chinese call this grain-splattered road the "Yellow Road," which to us, is the path of the Zodiac.

* * * * *

Virgo is found by following the curve of the handle of the "Big Dipper" in Ursa Major and extending it through Arcturus (Alpha Boötis), the bright orangish star, on to Spica (Alpha Virginis). Spica is a bright, very hot blue-white star like Rigel (Beta Orionis) and seems brighter than it is because there are no other bright stars near it. Spica signifies the "Ear of Wheat" held in the Virgin's hand. It also stands for the "Horn" or "Spike."

Virgo is chock full of galaxies which unfortunately are not bright enough to see except in a telescope. These galaxies form the densest accumulation of matter in our part of the universe. This group is a member of an immense gathering of galaxies called the Local Supercluster.

CANCER THE CRAB AND THE BEEHIVE CLUSTER

Although Cancer the Crab is the least conspicuous constellation in the Zodiac, it was well known as early as 4000 B.C. In Chaldea it was called the "Gate of Men" through which the souls in heaven descended and entered as humans. It was also construed in Babylonia as the "Tortoise." The Egyptian chronicles later identified it with their sacred beetle, the "Scarabaeus." The designs on the back of the beetle were believed to stand for the rays of the Sun and the dung pellets, in which the beetle laid its eggs, symbolized birth, resurrection and immortality. In the 13th century it was pictured in Europe as a "crayfish" which was changed 300 years later into the "Greater and Lesser Lobsters," the smaller lobster more like the size of a shrimp. The Tibetians followed the more square shape of the Crab, depicting it as a "Frog" which included Pollux (Alpha Geminorum).

In the Greek myths the celestial Crab tries to prevent Hercules from killing Hydra the Water Snake, but the Crab is crushed under his foot while it is pinching Hercules's toes. Juno honored its bravery or perhaps its pugnacious-ness by placing it in the sky.

The small square of stars, which are centrally located in the Crab, represented the "Mouth" or "Muzzle of the Lion" to the Arabs. This enormous constellation which also included Coma Berenices, was later separated from the Crab. In subsequent years the Hebrews, Greeks and Romans arranged the four stars in the center of the Crab into a manger with the two lower or eastern stars forming the "Aselli," the "Northern and Southern Asses or Don-keys."

* * * * *

The Crab may be found by forming a lopsided "V" from Pollux (Alpha Geminorum) and Procyon (Alpha Canis Minoris) which intersects the Crab on the left hand or northern leg. The stars of the Crab are dim — after all, the Crab was stomped on by Hercules — but its chief attraction, M44 (NGC-2632), the Praesepe or Beehive clus-ter, resides inside the four-starred "Manger." Before the invention of the telescope the Beehive was known as the "Little Cloud" or "Little Mist" or "Whirling Cloud." It was frequently used as an indicator of rain when it became dim or disappeared. The Beehive looks like a fuzzy patch until binoculars reveal it teeming with stars that indeed vividly suggest a beehive alive with glittering bees. Be sure to include M44 in your spring treasure chest.

LEO THE LION AND THE SICKLE ASTERISM OR CAPTAIN HOOK'S HOOK

Leo the Lion rises in profile below the Crab, dominat-ing the spring sky screen. Its popular asterism, the "Sickle," rises first and looks like a reversed question mark. or Captain Hook's "Hook." The rectangular-shaped body follows with a bright triangle forming the tail. The ancient figure of the Lion was enormous, encompassing parts of Gemini, Cancer, Virgo, Libra and others. The Lion's muzzle extended to the "Beehive" in Cancer and its long curling tail ended in Coma Berenices. Denebola (Beta Leonis) marked the base of the tail, but today is the tail's end.

An old Babylonian story relates how Pyramus and Thisbe, young lovers who live in adjacent apartment buildings, wanted to get married. Their parents refused permission and would not allow them to see each other, so the couple met secretly. One day Pyramus faxed a note to Thisbe asking her to meet him at the Zoo under the mulberry tree by the lion's pit after work. Thisbe arrived first and watched with fascination as Leo the Lion devoured his evening meal. As she was leaning over the pit, a stiff breeze blew her scarf down on top of the Lion. Leo angrily pounced on it and splattered blood all over it. Momentarily forgetting about Pyramus, Thisbe dashed away to the administrator's office to try to get her scarf back before the Zoo closed.

Meanwhile Pyramus arrived and recoiled in horror when he saw the scarf, believing that Thisbe had fallen into the pit and been killed. He blamed himself for her death because he asked her to meet him there. Pulling out his knife, he stabbed himself and fell beneath the mulberry tree. Thisbe returned, unsuccessful in finding someone to retrieve her scarf and found Pyramus lying dead. She screamed in agony, snatched the knife from his body and plunged it into her heart. The blood from the lovers soaked into the ground, staining the roots of the tree which caused the mulberries to change from white to red and then to black.

When the parents discovered this heartrending and needless tragedy, they united the two lovers by burying them side by side. Thisbe's scarf was forgotten and placed in the trash by the zoo cleaners. Columba the Dove happened to see the scarf and took it up to the stars where it now flutters in the constellation Coma Berenices.

The Babylonians also saw Leo as a huge guard dog whose head is marked by the beginning of the "Sickle" and one of its great paws by Regulus (Alpha Leonis). Various Indian tribes of northern Brazil pictured it as an enormous "Crayfish" which ignored the "Sickle" and Regulus. It was also Tauna, the God of Thunder and Lightning, shown holding up an immense cudgel. The Chinese incorporated the "Sickle" into their "Rain Dragon," but no other stars of the constellation were used.

* * * * *

The end of the "Sickle" is marked by the first-magnitude star Regulus (Alpha Leonis) or Cor Leonis, meaning "Heart of the Lion." For at least 3000 years before our day it was believed that Regulus ruled the heavens and was the leader of the Four Royal Stars, Fomalhaut (Alpha Piscis Austrini), Aldebaran (Alpha Tauri) and Antares (Alpha Scorpii). Regulus is a triple star, the 20th brightest, and is often occulted or momentarily blocked from our view by the Moon.

Denebola (Beta Leonis) comes from the Arabic word meaning "Tail of the Lion." It is a multiple star of different colors.

The Leonids, a famous meteor shower, occurs during November. Refer to Appendix III for details.

COMA BERENICES — BERENICE'S HAIR

Coma Berenices is one of the delicate beauties of the sky and has been exquisitely described as "gossamers spangled with dewdrops." In binoculars you may easily imagine it as the tuft of Leo the Lion's tail or Thisbe's veil described under Leo, or as the magnificent amber hair of Berenice, the enchanting wife of King Ptolemy Soter. How her hair ended up in the heavens is a touching tale.

Berenice II, a queen of Egypt for whom the constellation was named, had recently married Ptolemy when he had to go to war in the Persian Gulf. As his absence extended into months, she became increasingly distraught, and fearing for his life, beseeched Venus, the Goddess of Love, that if Venus would return Ptolemy unharmed, Berenice would sacrifice her magnificent hair. When Ptolemy calls her on his cellular phone that he is coming home at last, she cuts off her golden locks. Ptolemy arrives to find a bald-headed wife and is very upset about her appearance! He knows, of course, that the hair will all grow out again, but in the meantime, he can only gaze at her hair which Berenice has placed on the altar in the temple of Venus.

The following morning Ptolemy goes to the temple to look at Berenice's hair and is outraged when he discovers that it is gone. He whips out his Uzi and is about to waste the priests who were responsible for guarding it when the Court Astronomer stops him.

"Cool it, King!" he cries. "Berenice's hair has been enshrined in the heavens for all the world to see." There it remains, laid out neatly in delicate strands, glistening with tiny diamonds.

* * * * *

Berenice's hair is aptly named, for its delicate strings of stars appear as strands of hair laid out on black velvet. To find Berenice's Hair, sight on a line from Alkaid (Eta Ursae Majoris) at the end of the handle of the "Big Dipper" to Cor Caroli (Alpha Canum Venaticorum) and on to Denebola (Beta Leonis), the tail end of Leo. The Hair lies about halfway between Cor Caroli and Denebola.

Coma Berenice contains Mel 111, the exquisite open star cluster whose stars are thought to have been born from a single cloud of gas and dust and are still loosely bound by gravity. Mel 111, named for astronomer P. J. Melotte, spreads out six degrees in diameter, resembling a spray of pearls, an appropriate adornment for Berenice's Hair. In the direction of this cluster is one of the densest concentrations of external galaxies and the galactic north pole of the Milky Way Galaxy.

HYDRA THE FEMALE WATER SNAKE

Rearing its four-starred oval head to the south of the "Sickle" in Leo the Lion, Hydra the Female Water Snake slithers toward the south, twisting and turning just like a snake is supposed to do. Hydra is the largest and longest of the eighty-eight constellations and although it contains mostly faint stars, it is not hard to trace.

Hydra was supposedly the snake with numerous heads that Hercules had to kill in order to steal the golden apples of the Hesperides. Hercules mightily whacked off Hydra's heads but two would grow in place of the one he had just severed. Fortunately Hercules had a buddy who burned the stump of each head as he cut them off so that no more heads would continue to grow.

Another story involving Hydra with Corvus the Greedy Crow who tried to use Hydra as a scapegoat is found under Corvus.

* * * * *

Hydra's little head, consisting of four faint stars, is easy to spot because of its distinctive oval shape. It suggested other figures such as a flag to the Jaina of India. Hindus thought it was a potter's wheel. The Chinese saw the "Willow Branch" of the third house of the Red Bird which symbolized summer. This was the time when sacrifices were made to the ancestors. A willow branch was planted by the temple doors and depending upon which way the branch leaned, the sacramental feasts were prepared in that direction.

To find Hydra's head either look directly below Procyon (Alpha Canis Minoris) a little more than a handspan or take a direct line from Castor (Beta Geminorum) through Pollux (Alpha Gem) which intersects it. Continuing the line will bring you to Hydra's brightest star, Alphard (Alpha Hydrae). Alphard comes from the Arabic name, the "Solitary One in the Serpent." Hydra continues down past Corvus the Crow which perches on its back and ends at Gamma Hya.

M48 (NGC-2548), an open star cluster, glows mistily from the western boundary of Hydra four degrees southeast of Zeta Monocerotis. Binoculars will reveal a few of its arches and strings of faint stars.

CORVUS THE GREEDY CROW AND CRATER THE BEAKER

Corvus the Crow is a bright kite-shaped constellation of five stars in the southeast. The reason why crows are black and have such horrible voices is all due to Corvus becoming too greedy one day on an errand for Apollo.

One day Apollo gets thirsty and asks Corvus, then a beautiful white crow, to go down and fetch him a Heineken. Corvus flies down with the beer stein (otherwise known as Crater the Beaker) to the bar where Hydra the Female Water Snake hangs out. Corvus is about to get the beer when he spies a tree full of ripe, juicy mangos. Corvus likes nothing better than mangos, so he parks himself in that mango tree and gorges himself the rest of the day. When he finally remembers what he was supposed to do, he fills the stein with beer and flies back to Apollo.

Corvus explains that he is late because Hydra prevented him from getting to the bar but Apollo isn't fooled. He changes Corvus's silver feathers to black and his beautiful song into a croak.

* * * * *

Corvus stands out in a dim section of the southeast sky and is easily found by continuing the arc of the handle of the "Big Dipper" in Ursa Major to Arcturus (Alpha Boötis), then on to Spica (Alpha Virginis) and curving upward. Many figures have been seen in this tidy group; in India, a hand; with the Axtecs, the tail of a scorpion; in Europe and America, the "Cutter's Mainsail." Others are an elephant, a heron, a cart and a kangaroo. The Navajos called Corvus the "Man with Feet Spread Apart." Corvus perches toward the end of Hydra with the Beaker just above it. Its dim stars form a wine cup according to the Persians or an amphora to the Spanish. The contents of the Beaker slosh out when Hydra slinks below the western horizon.

Greedy Corvus the Crow
Pigs Out Under the Mango Tree

SPRING SECTION OF ARGO AND THE SOUTHERN SKY

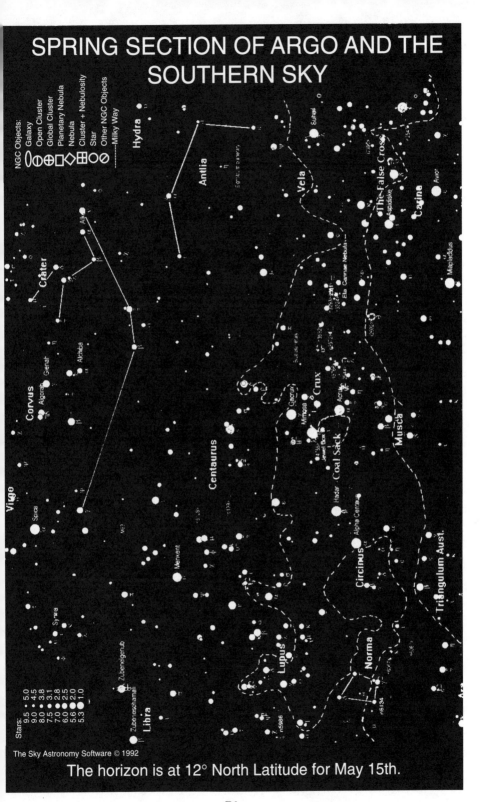

The horizon is at 12° North Latitude for May 15th.

The Sky Astronomy Software © 1992

THE ETA CARINAE FAMILY

In the Springtime southern sky the "False Cross" asterism on the border of Carina the Keel and Vela the Sail stands upright. A little over one handspan to the east of the "False Cross" reside the finest collection of nebulae and star clusters in the southern sky. At first you may notice what appears to be little puffy white clouds lying a handspan or so above the horizon. But wait! These little white clouds don't move! The brightest of these clouds, IC 2602, is a brilliant blob of stars known as the Theta Carinae cluster. To locate IC 2602 extend a line through the cross bar in the "False Cross" and head slightly over one handspan eastward. IC 2602 is the lowest of the clouds to the horizon and is a magnificent cluster.

Directly north of this jewel is the queen of emission nebula, NGC-3372 called the Eta Carinae or Keyhole Nebula, the largest of the cloud-like gems. It is a huge glowing nebula and like M42 (NGC-1976), the Orion Nebula, is the number one object to observe in the southern sky and log in your treasure chest. Entombed in this glistening teardrop is Eta Carinae, a star that periodically brightens or dims. It is presently below naked-eye visibility.

Many clusters surround the Eta Carinae Nebula such as NGC-3293, a tight but rich cluster about a degree above Eta and IC 2581, 2° to the northwest. Particularly stunning is the bright swirl of NGC-3114 about half a handspan west of Eta. NGC-3114 delights the imagination because of its intriguing, knotty-looking appearance. NGC-3532, another open cluster, is a bright splotch 3° east-northeast of Eta. Tangles of chains and rings charm your eye in binoculars. Take many nights to peruse among these wondrous southern temples of light.

CRUX THE SOUTHERN CROSS

Five thousand years ago the stars of Crux the Southern Cross were part of the northern European sky. Due to precession, the wobble of the Earth as it rotates on its axis, the Cross is now seen in the northern tropics and the Southern Hemisphere. Undoubtedly its four bright stars were an important figure in ancient times but there are no known records of it as a separate entity from Centaurus the Centaur. Allusions to its stars did not appear until the famous poet Alighieri Dante wrote the *Purgatorio* and after sea explorers of the 15th century wrote accounts of its resplendent configuration. The Italian navigator Andreas Corsali may have been the first to describe it in 1516, but centuries before that during the time of Claudius Ptolemy when he catalogued 48 constellations around A.D. 150, the Southern Cross was pictured as part of the hind feet of Centaurus.

To the people of the south Crux was the Southern Celestial Clock. Because the Cross is almost perpendicular when it culminates which is the moment when it reaches the meridian, you may easily observe the motion of the heavens which advances four minutes a day.

Before Christianity spread to the southern latitudes, the constellation was not seen as a cross. Among the Solomon Islands it was a knee cap protector or sometimes a net for catching Palolo worms. It was a fish or ray to other islanders and when Gamma Centauri, the bright star above it was included, the Australian Aborigines saw it as the "Fishing Spear" or the "Eagle's Foot."

* * * * *

Crux, the smallest of the constellations, is a mere six degrees long and looks more like a badly made kite than a cross, but its lopsided figure does not detract from its riveting beauty. It is just east of the cloud-like array of nebulae and star clusters a handspan or so above the southern horizon.

Acrux (Alpha Crucis), the foot star of the Cross, was once the Pole Star of the South but now that the South Pole is almost 28 degrees south of it, another star has been selected because it is much nearer.

Crux is enmeshed in the Milky Way Stream and contains the much acclaimed star cluster NGC-4755. It is known as the "Jewel Box" because of its multicolored stars and is tucked under Mimosa (Beta Crucis), the eastern star of the cross bar by its southeastern side. Between and east of Mimosa (Beta Cru) and Acrux (Alpha Cru) is the pear-shaped dark nebula, the "Coal Sack," once called the "Black Magellanic Cloud" or "Magellan's Spot." In the 19th century astronomers thought that black spots like the "Coal Sack" were holes or windows through which we could look into outer space. Today we know that the "Coal Sack" is dark matter which blocks the starlight behind it. It was just this sort of dark spot that some native Americans believed were holes in the huge black bearskin which was the sky.

CENTAURUS THE CENTAUR AND THE OMEGA CENTAURI CLUSTER

Centaurus, which once contained the Southern Cross, stands above and eastward of Crux the Southern Cross. Its profusion of bright stars presents no distinctive pattern so one must navigate by star-hopping or creating figures.

The Classical Greek and Roman view of Centaurus is that of Chiron, a gentle and kind teacher of poetry, music, math and medicine. Chiron was not the wild savage beast usually depicted because he had a different parentage. His father Cronus, king of the Titans, was seducing the sea nymph Philyra, but when caught in the act by his wife Rhea, turned himself into a horse and beat feet. Consequently Philyra bore his hybrid son Chiron. Chiron came to a tragic end by being accidentally killed by Hercules when one of his poisoned arrows struck him in the knee. Chiron was depicted as sometimes holding a spear over one shoulder from which a hare and a goat or wolf were suspended as an offering.

* * * * *

Centaurus is unwieldy and sometimes drawn as a misshaped rectangle between Hydra the Female Water Snake and Crux. Its northeastern end is pointed like a hat ending at Menkent (Theta Centauri). The southwestern end representing its legs bracket the Southern Cross. The forelegs contain the bright stellar beacons Rigil Kentaurus (Alpha Centauri) and Hadar (Beta Cen) which act as pointers to Crux.

Alpha Centauri is the third brightest star and its companion Proxima Centauri is the closest star to us. Proxima is a "flare star," a red dwarf whose light can fluctuate drastically in only minutes. The flares are unpredictable and the phenomena is not well understood.

Hadar (Beta Cen) is the tenth brightest star and was known as the Horse's Belly by the Chinese. Both Alpha and Beta were sometimes called Wezen and Hadar meaning "Ground" and "Weight" as were stars in Argo the Ship, Columba the Dove and Canis Major. In Aboriginal lore they are the "Two Brothers"; to the Bushmen of South Africa, the "Two Men that Once Were Lions." Navigators know Alpha as Rigil Kentaurus.

The brightest and largest of globular clusters in the sky, Omega Centauri (NGC-5139) nestles above Epsilon, the first bright star above Hadar. A line drawn from Hadar (Beta Centauri) through Epsilon and continued about the same distance will bring you to this giant powder puff. It is dazzling in a telescope and compared to any other globular, beats them all hollow.

About four degrees due north of Omega is NGC-5128, a lenticular galaxy also dubbed Centaurus A. This bright active galaxy appears in binoculars as two identical semi-circles with a dark band between them. It is a violent emitter of radio waves and is suspected of harboring the Godzilla of black holes.

Swishing between Crux and Carina is the tail of Centaurus shown by a pretty little tangle of stars sporting a sparkling diamond necklace. Two open clusters, NGC-3766 and IC 2944, stud the necklace within this dazzling little pocket of gems.

LUPUS THE WOLF

Like Centaurus, Lupus the Wolf is a constellation of bright stars with few distinctive patterns. Try studying it in small parcels, ferreting out its peculiarities and creating your own loops, triangles and other images.

Lupus is a very old constellation and it is thought that the Babylonians called it the "Wild Dog." To the Greeks and Romans it was a wild beast of some sort that the Centaur held as an offering to Ara the Altar. The Persians depicted Lupus as a leopard or lioness while West Europeans considered it as a wolf.

* * * * *

Separating Lupus from Centaurus in order to find NGC-5986, the brightest globular cluster in Lupus is a real challenge. Find Menkent (Theta Centauri) the most northern bright star in Centaurus and move a bit less than two handspans southeast to Eta Centauri, the bright star which forms the eastern side of Centaurus. Beta Lupi is a mere four fingers further east. From Beta sight a line northeasterly to Delta Lupi and continue onward about the same distance to intersect NGC-5986, a large misty ball of light.

NORMA THE CARPENTER'S SQUARE

Norma is one of the tools which de Lacaille placed near Circinus, the Drawing Compass and Triangulum Australe, the Southern Triangle. Normally, Norma is skipped over because its star patterns are dim, but its saving grace is its three bright open clusters.

* * * * *

Norma is tucked beside the southeast side of Lupus. Alpha and Beta Centauri almost point to NGC-6087, the brightest star cluster. On a line drawn through Alpha and Beta go about one and a half handspans east and then move directly north about three fingers to intersect the cluster. Almost the same magnitude but a smaller fuzzy knot is NGC-6067 directly north about three fingers above NGC-6087. To find NGC-6134, the third cluster, move northeasterly about half a handspan up through a trio of stars. NGC-6134, a splash of stars lies above them. Excellent binoculars may show NGC-6152, a dimmer but larger cluster the diameter of the Moon. If you get all these clusters under your belt, you can count yourself as a star-seeker of some skill.

MUSCA THE ONLY FLY IN THE SKY

Musca used to be Musca Australis, the Southern Fly because Musca Borealis, another insect representing either a bee or wasp was once part of four stars in Aries the Ram. Today it is obsolete and Musca flies along under Crux the Southern Cross.

In Greek legends Musca may have been the sky fly that was sent by Jupiter to bite the rump of Pegasus the Winged Horse. His rider Bellerophon, in a reckless mood, urged Pegasus to fly too close to Mount Olympus, home of Jupiter and his family. When Musca bit Pegasus, it reared and

Bellerophon fell to Earth, never permitted to ride Pegasus again to explore the heavens.

Another story involving Musca tells of Io, the beautiful priestess who Jupiter seduces and impregnates. Juno, his suspicious wife, is no air head and is about to do Io in, but Jupiter protects Io by changing her into a white heifer. Juno is not about to be outwitted and sends Musca to torment the heifer. Argus the Giant with the one hundred eyes is commanded to prevent Io from escaping. Jupiter wins in the end by sending Mercury to give Argus some grass which puts him in a stupor. All of his one hundred eyes slowly close and Jupiter changes Io back into a woman again.

* * * * *

Musca lies less than a handspan directly below Crux the Southern Cross. It is a tidy group of six dim stars and with some imagination may be construed as a pesky fly.

Three clusters glow softly in Musca. Two degrees south of Acrux (Alpha Cru) NGC-4463, an open cluster, perches on the western edge of the Coal Sack. NGC-4372, a globular cluster, is one-half a degree southwest of Gamma Muscae, the western foot while NGC-4833, another globular cluster, perches one degree northeast of Delta Mus, the eastern foot.

VIII

The Spring Obscure Constellations

*A*long dim thread of stars lies between the paws of the Great Bear (Ursa Major) in the north, Auriga the Herdsman, Gemini the Twins and Leo the Lion in the south. From this string two constellations were formed by the Polish astronomer, Johannes Hevelius in the 17th century. The upper part of the strand, the Lynx, may have stood for the treacherous King Lyncus of Scythia who extended his hospitality to his guest, Triptolemus, the chariot driver of Ceres, the Goddess of Agriculture, and then plotted to kill him while he slept. As he was about to slay Triptolemus, Ceres changed Lyncus into a Lynx and relegated him to the sky where he is so obscure, few notice him, an appropriate punishment for his savagery.

Leo Minor the Little Lion continues the string of stars below the Great Bear's hind paws and north of Leo the Lion. So unlion-like is he that one might believe that the Little Lion has been squashed flat by the Bear.

Between Leo and Hydra the Female Water Snake lies another creation of Hevelius named the Sextans which commemorated the handsome large sextant which was destroyed when his observatory burned down. It is a pity that such an important instrument was not placed among brighter stars so that the constellation could be easily detected.

The Abbe Nicholas Louis de Lacaille sneaked Antlia the Air Pump in between the middle of Hydra across from Crater and Vela the Sail. It contains S-Antliae, a noteworthy variable star which changes its brightness within one of the shortest periods known, a mere seven and a half hours.

The Abbe continued to externalize the tools of the explorers of the southern oceans and placed Norma the Carpenter's Square east of Lupus the Wolf, and Circinus the Drawing Compass below Lupus and east of Centaurus.

Johannes Bayer placed another instrument, Triangulum Australe, the Southern Triangle, below Norma and east of Circinus, attributing its origin to the southern voyagers. Below the Southern Triangle he put the southern circumpolar Apus, the Bird of Paradise, another constellation introduced to Europe by the Magellan expedition. This magnificently-attired bird perches upside down on the Southern Triangle, its long tail feathers almost tickling the forefeet of Centaurus to the east of the Southern Cross. This bird was known to the Chinese as the "Curious Sparrow," the "Fire Bird" and the "Little Wonder Bird."

Below Musca resides the Chamaeleon clinging upside down to a branch, his eye riveted on the Fly. If Bayer had placed the Chamaeleon just a couple of degrees closer to Musca, there would surely be no insect in the sky!

Your Spring Treasure Chest

Constellation	Type of Object Clus, Gal, Neb	Binocs/eye (Type)	Description Shape, Color Brightness	Comments

Your Spring Treasure Chest

DATE	TIME	LOCATION	WEATHER			OBJECT NAME
			Clouds?	Haze?	Moon Phase	And No.

IX

Summer Sky Preview

Commanding the northern summer sky is Draco the Sleepy Dragon, twisting between the Bears and the Hunters. Draco's eye is fixed on Vega in Lyra the Vulture, the brightest summer star, as if hoping for a tasty meal.

The magnificent Milky Way Stream cuts majestically across the sky separating Hercules, Rambo of the Skies and the heroic Serpent Bearer, Ophiuchus, from the three summer birds, Lyra the Vulture, Cygnus the Swan and Aquila the Eagle. The Vulture has kept his wings dry as all vultures should, but the Swan and Eagle frolic in the Stream oblivious to Vulpecula the Little Fox and to Sagittarius the Archer in the south.

Scorpius, the villain who does in Orion the Hunter, rears high in the southeast, but Ophiuchus stands nearby, ready to stomp on it. The Archer also has it in for the Scorpion with his bow and arrow drawn, pointing at its heart. Libra the Scales stands serenely above Scorpius, feeling smug for having stolen the claws of Scorpius.

Separating the Milky Way Stream into channels from Cygnus toward the south is a long island of dark nebula called the Great Rift. Great swirls of star shoals fill the Stream, particularly in Scutum the Shield down through Sagittarius and Scorpius where star clusters and bright knots of nebulae are cluttered. Two splendid nebulae, M8

(NGC-6523) and M20 (NGC-6514), the Lagoon and Trifid, stun the stargazer along with the sparkling star clusters M6 (NGC-6405) and M7 (NGC-6475) between Sagittarius and Scorpius. Even the longest summer nights do not allow enough hours to enjoy all these wonders.

SUMMERTIME SKY LOOKING NORTH

The Sky Astronomy Software © 1992

The horizon is at 12° North Latitude for July 1st..

85

SUMMERTIME SKY LOOKING EAST

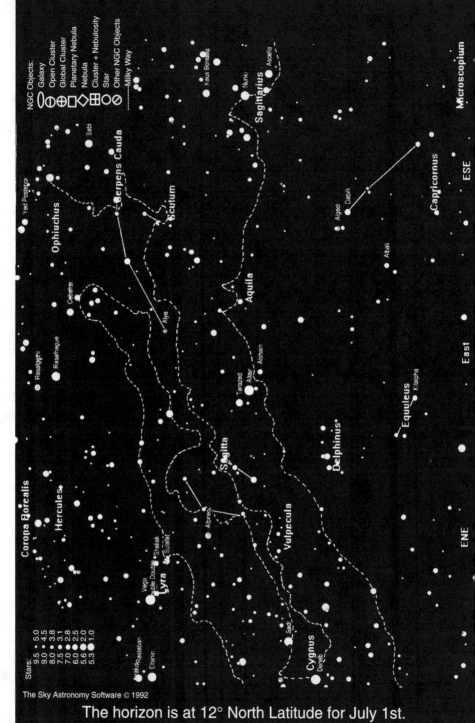

The Sky Astronomy Software © 1992

The horizon is at 12° North Latitude for July 1st.

SUMMERTIME SKY LOOKING SOUTH

NGC Objects:
-) Galaxy
- (Open Cluster
- ⊕ Global Cluster
- □ Planetary Nebula
- ◇ Nebula
- ⊞ Cluster + Nebulosity
- ○ Star
- ⊘ Other NGC Objects
- ---- Milky Way

Stars:
- 9.5 • 5.0
- 9.0 • 4.5
- 8.0 • 3.8
- 7.5 • 3.1
- 7.0 • 2.8
- 6.0 • 2.5
- 5.6 • 2.0
- 5.3 • 1.0

The Sky Astronomy Software © 1992

The horizon is at 12° North Latitude for July 1st.

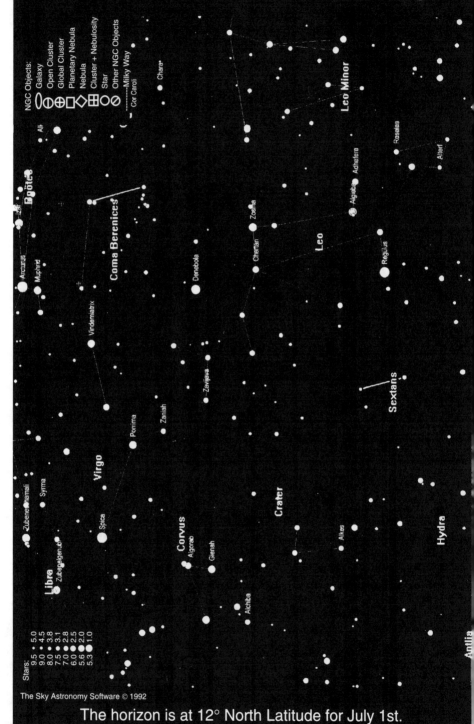

SUMMERTIME SKY LOOKING WEST

NGC Objects:
Galaxy
Open Cluster
Global Cluster
Planetary Nebula
Nebula
Cluster + Nebulosity
Star
Other NGC Objects
Milky Way

Stars:
9.5 • 5.0
9.0 • 4.5
8.0 • 3.8
7.5 • 3.1
7.0 • 2.8
6.0 • 2.5
5.6 • 2.0
5.3 • 1.0

Leo Minor
Rasalas
Alterf
Chara
Cor Caroli
Boötes
Ali
Coma Berenices
Zosma
Denebola
Arcturus
Muphrid
Algieba
Adhafera
Leo
Regulus
Vindemiatrix
Chertan
Zavijava
Zaniah
Sextans
Porrima
Virgo
Syrma
Crater
Zubeneschamali
Spica
Hydra
Corvus
Alkes
Zubenelgenubi
Libra
Algorab
Gienah
Alchiba
Antlia

The Sky Astronomy Software © 1992

The horizon is at 12° North Latitude for July 1st.

DRACO THE SLEEPY DRAGON

Draco winds between the Great and Little Bears, rearing high to glare at Vega in Lyra the Vulture or Lute. Draco is the dragon that was commanded by Juno, the wife of Jupiter, to guard the golden apple tree that was given to her as a wedding present. Hercules, the Rambo of the skies, was sent to steal the golden apples. Draco was known to have a sweet tooth, so Hercules whipped up a chocolate milk shake and put a sleeping draught in it. Draco slurped it up with gusto, fell asleep and Hercules snuck off with the apples. Fortunately Draco wasn't punished and still has a permanent place between the Great and Little Bears as the eighth largest constellation.

In another version Hercules slays the sleepy Dragon. A third legend describes a feud between Draco and Minerva, the Goddess of Wisdom. Minerva grabs Draco by its ugly tail and hurtles it into the heavens. Poor Draco gets all tangled up in knots and before it can untwist itself, it strikes the dome of the stars overhead and instantly freezes because it is so close to the North Pole.

In the eastern cultures the Dragon is identified with evil and darkness and is responsible for causing eclipses of the Sun or Moon. During an eclipse the Dragon devours the Sun or Moon and it is up to the people to scare it away by making as much noise as possible so that it will spit one or the other out.

The Arabs had a totally different image of the Dragon's stars, believing that four female camels stood where its head is, to protect a baby camel from the attack of two hyenas seen near the end of the Dragon.

* * * * *

Trace the Dragon by starting at the tail end which begins slightly west of and between the line made by the pointer stars, Dubhe (Alpha Ursae Majoris) and Merak (Beta UMa) in the Big Dipper to Polaris, the North Star. The third faint star from the tail end is Thuban (Alpha Draconis). About 2750 B.C. Thuban was the Pole Star and may have been brighter than it is today. When some of the Egyptian pyramids were built, Thuban was used to determine the north alignments and passageways and it shone directly down these shafts.

From Thuban (Alpha) the body of Draco curves down below Kochab (Beta Ursa Minoris) and Pherkad (Gamma UMi) which form the end of the Little Dipper asterism into a clutch of eight bright stars which form the final knot. Moving back up from this tangle the neck stretches up and terminates at the head which is sometimes called the Lozenge.

Draco's head is formed by four stars. The brightest is Eltanin (Gamma Draconis), the Dragon's right eye or nostril. It is a double star easily split with the naked eye. Forming the head or left eye is Rastaban (Beta) along with Grumium (Xi) and Nu.

Between June and September at least three meteor showers come from Draco, appropriately symbolizing flames or meteors shooting from its mouth. Consult Appendix III for meteor shower details.

Draco the Sleepy Dragon Guards the Golden Apples

THE SUMMER BIRDS

NGC Objects:
Galaxy
Open Cluster
Global Cluster
Planetary Nebula
Nebula
Cluster + Nebulosity
Star
Other NGC Objects
Milky Way

Scutum
B111 B119a
M11 = NGC6705 Wild Duck cluster

Aquila
Alshain
Altair
Tarazed B142 µ
B143

Equuleus
Kitalpha
α
β

Ophiuchus
Yed Posterior
Cebalrai
Rasalhague
α
Rasalgethi

2 Alya

Delphinus
M15

Sagitta
Harvard 20
M71
Cr399

Great Rift

Vulpecula

Hercules
Great Clstr in Hercules
M13
M92

Corona Borealis
Alphecca
Nusakan
Seginus

Lyra
Vega
Double Double
Sheliak
Sulafat

Summer Triangle

Northern Cross

Cygnus
Deneb
Albireo
Sadr
M29
n6871
n7000

Draco
Eltanin
Rastaban
Ainalrai
Grumium
Alrakis
Edasich
Aldhibah
Thuban

Alderamin
Alfirk
Errai

East
Sadalsuud
Enif
M2

ENE

LacNE

NNE

Stars:
9.5 — 5.0
9.0 — 4.5
8.0 — 3.8
7.5 — 3.1
7.0 — 2.8
6.0 — 2.5
5.6 — 2.0
5.3 — 1.0

The Sky Astronomy Software © 1992

The horizon is at 12° North Latitude for July 1st.

91

LYRA THE VULTURE

Prominent in the northeast is Vega (Alpha Lyrae), the fifth brightest star in the sky. Vega is in Lyra the Lyre or Harp which is also known as the Vulture. As a lyre it represents the first ever made when, according to the Greek myth, Mercury found an empty tortoise shell, fastened some string to it and with his magic touch, produced exquisite sounds. Apollo was so enchanted that he asked Mercury to trade it for a pair of winged sandals and a staff or caduceus, the emblem of life and death. Mercury gave it to Orpheus, Apollo's son, who was such a fine musician that he could quiet the sea and even charm the rocks. Orpehus was unjustly killed by some jealous women whom he scorned in favor of playing his harp. Obviously the poor man didn't have his priorities right! The spurned ladies threw the harp into the river but a vulture scooped it out and placed in the heavens.

* * * * *

It's hard to miss brilliant blue-white Vega in the northeast, but if in doubt, look for the distinctive four-starred head of Draco the Dragon in which Eltanin (Gamma Draconis) points straight to it. The Arabs called Vega the Swooping Stone Eagle of the Desert and the word means "plunging one." Vega was the North Star between 11,000 and 12,000 B.C. and will occupy that position again in the year 13,500. It is a popular navigation star and it forms the Summer Triangle along with Deneb (Alpha Cygni) and Altair (Alpha Aquilae). Northeast or one pinkie to the left of Vega is Epsilon Lyrae, a double star. Each of the pair is a double star, so you're actually seeing a double-double. Two fingers slightly southeast of Vega is Delta Lyrae, a beautiful double of blue-white and orangish stars in binoculars.

Lyra is a small constellation but is distinctive with its pairs of double stars. It is more easily seen as a harp than as the Vulture. As the Vulture, it flies along the western bank of the Milky Way Stream. The Persians saw a tortoise or a clay tablet and the Romans, a vase. As a compact parallelogram, it also resembles a rudder with Vega marking the tiller.

The Lyrid meteor shower occurs the third week of April. For more details consult Appendix III.

CYGNUS THE SWAN

Flying through the Milky Way Stream, its long neck pointing toward the southeast, Cygnus the Swan is also known as the Northern Cross, its cross bar formed by the outspread wings.

A story involving the Swan is about the seduction of Leda, the wife of the King of Sparta, by Jupiter. As Leda was washing in a pool, Jupiter looked down and fell in love with her. Masquerading as a majestic swan, he swam up to her so that she could stroke his beautiful white feathers and when she did, Jupiter captured her. From this union Pollux, the immortal twin of Gemini and Helen of Troy were conceived. Leda also lay with her husband that night and conceived Castor, the other twin of Gemini and Klytamnestra. This meant that although Pollux and Castor were twins, Castor was mortal while Pollux was not, which caused the problem related under Gemini.

* * * * *

Cygnus, the second Summer Bird, is so immersed in the Milky Way Stream that you have to look carefully for its cross-like shape. Not that its stars aren't bright, but that there is such a profusion of them that it takes perseverence to sort them all out. To land just a little southeast of the Swan's wings or the cross bar, take a line through Rastaban (Beta Draconis) and Eltanin (Gamma Dra), the two brightest stars in the Dragon's head, into the Stream which will intersect the Swan's neck. Another way is to go about one handspan below bright Vega (Alpha Lyrae) in the northeast, cross the dark lane of nebula where you enter the bright part of the Stream where Cygnus flies.

Cygnus is like a kaleidoscope, chock full of loops, arcs, swiggles and other figures. Get acquainted with Cygnus by first moving northerly to Deneb (Alpha Cygni), the most distant of the first-magnitude stars. Deneb, an Arabic word meaning the "Hen's Tail," is about 2000 light years away and is an extraordinary luminous supergiant, hundreds of times brighter than our Sun. It is only because Deneb is so far away that it appears dimmer than Sirius (Alpha Canis Majoris) or Canopus (Alpha Carinae).

Before exploring the area from Deneb to Albireo (Beta Cygni), the swan's head, backtrack about four fingers northwesterly with binoculars until a bright triangular patch of stars comes into view. This is M39 (NGC-7092), a fine, messy object worthy of your treasure chest. M39 is an arresting open star cluster which stands out amidst the entanglements of stars surrounding it.

Now you are in position to move toward Deneb (Alpha) to find NGC-7000, the North America Nebula, in binoculars. This large emission nebula looks like a misty patch resembling the continent just southeast of Deneb. Dark nebulae on either side make its contours stand out. The North America Nebula is a fine prize for the diligent stargazer. If you don't get it at first, keep trying and some night it will pop out so clearly that you'll wonder why you didn't see it right away.

Pause now, using only your peepers, to see the Great Rift, the lone dark island which separates the Milky Way Stream into two branches. The Rift starts immediately south of Deneb, dividing the Stream until it merges with the western bank.

To appreciate this magnificent star-studded area of Cygnus, play the ink blot game. Look at the shoals of stars as if they were schools of tiny fish. Then invert your vision as you would with ink blots and notice the fingers of dark nebulae that intrically divide the fish. New patterns will suddenly emerge. Look at the dark nebula beside the eastern seaboard of the North America Nebula and how both its form and the dark nebula tucked beside it become distinctive.

Take a breather and shift to Sadr (Gamma), the center of the cross bar and the heart of the Swan. Sadr is practically smothered with the enormous emission nebula IC-1318 which will make your imagination go berserk!

Moving south hardly a finger away is another messy object, M29 (NGC-6913), a small knot of stars which would be more impressive if it wasn't awash with so many fantastic figures. A finger southwesterly of M29 is NGC-6871, another cluster far easier to pick out, only because it is brighter. Here one can also become aground for a spell picking out stellar images.

Before exiting Cygnus, amble toward Albireo (Beta), the head of the Swan, and you'll pass the gigantic vacuum cleaner of the spring sky, Cygnus X. Imagine it there, sucking in all that wanders near, gulping them down. From this mega-monstrous black hole, nothing can escape.

AGUILA THE EAGLE

Aquila, the third Summer Bird, flies toward Cygnus along the Milky Way Stream with its southern wing grazing the eastern bank. Aguila was the royal Eagle of Jupiter and performed various tasks for him such as killing Ophiuchus the Serpent Bearer and carrying and returning the thunderbolts that Jupiter hurled at his enemies. Aquila once had to snatch the beautiful Trojan boy Ganymede from Earth and transport him to the heavens where he became the celestial waiter for the gods. One gory myth exemplifies the terrible wrath of Jupiter when he has Prometheus, one of the Titans, chained to a mountain. Every day Jupiter sent Aquila to feast on the liver of Prometheus until Hercules finally put Prometheus out of his misery by setting him free.

In contrast to the Greek myths is the Korean version of the charming Chinese love story about Tchi-niu, the Weaving Princess who is represented by Vega (Alpha Lyrae) and Kien-niou, the herdsman by Altair (Alpha Aquilae). Tchi-niu and Kien-niou fall in love and are married. Kien-niou is changed into a prince and becoming heady with all of his newly acquired power, tries to tap the milk from the Milky Way, the Heavenly River, to divert it to malnourished stars. This act so angers his father-in-law that he separates the couple and permits them to meet only one day a year. Here they are, Altair, the Prince and Vega, his bride, separated by the Milky Way Stream.

How can they ever get across the Stream for even one day? With the help of some good-natured magpies which form a fluttering bridge, the Prince is able to cross over on the seventh day of the seventh Moon. A light, gentle rain falls all day, symbolizing the couple's happiness, but at dusk when Altair must leave, the rain becomes a torrent caused by their tears at his departure. Unfortunately, even the magpies suffer because they end up with bald heads when their feathers are worn off by the trampling feet of the Prince and his retinue. Happily, the feathers all grow back again by the next year.

* * * * *

One of the easiest ways to find the Eagle is to start at Vega (Alpha Lyrae), the brilliant star in the northeast and sight directly south to three stars in a row with its brightest star Altair (Alpha Aquilae), in the middle. The three might suggest Orion's Belt except that the western or topmost star, Tarazed (Gamma) is dim. With Alshain (Beta), the three form the chest of the Eagle.

The name Altair means "Rising One." Only 16 light years away, Altair is one of the closest stars to Earth and is remarkable because of its extremely rapid rotation, one of the fastest known. Altair rotates at roughly 160 miles per second, completing one rotation in $6^1/_2$ hours. Because of this rapid spinning the star probably has the shape of a flattened ellipsoid. It is the third point of the Summer Triangle.

As in Cygnus, the star patterns of Aguila are stunning in their great profusion and complexity through which dark nebulous matter intertwines. Two especially interesting dark nebulae are Barnard 142 and Barnard 143 about 3° northwest of Altair (Alpha). These nebulae form a stark "E", its three prongs pointing northwestward into a star cloud. Use your mental ink blot method to pluck it out with binoculars.

SCUTUM THE SHIELD

Scutum, the fifth smallest constellation, was placed in the sky by Johannes Hevelius in honor of King John III Sobiesci of Poland. The stars of Scutum are not brighter than fourth magnitude, but its two outstanding features make it one of the more frequently observed summer constellations.

Catching your eye at once is the stunning Scutum Star Cloud, a bright and distinctive shoal that crowns the rest of the starclouds that billow below it in Sagittarius. The western edge of the cloud stands out more clearly because of the dark nebulae snuggled beside it. Many dark nebulae course through it, Barnard 111 and Barnard 119a being the most prevalent. These are kidney-shaped patches which nearly combine at their southern ends.

Perching on the northern edge of the Scutum Star Cloud is M11 (NGC-6705), named the Wild Duck Cluster. M11 is an arrowhead-shaped globular cluster just south of B111 and B119a. If it doesn't pop out at you right away, scan the Stream with binoculars from Altair (Alpha Aquilae) and M11's bright, dense clump may arrest your eye just before you encounter the Scutum Star Cloud. Once you find it, you won't forget it!

VULPECULA THE LITTLE FOX AND THE COAT HANGER ASTERISM

Vulpecula is a small constellation about halfway between Vega (Alpha Lyrae) and Altair (Alpha Aquilae), two of the stars that form the Summer Triangle. Vulpecula used to be associated with a goose, but somehow the goose got lost, or more likely, ended up in a cooking pot and eaten by the Little Fox!

* * * * *

The stars of the Little Fox are too faint to excite the imagination with one notable exception, Collinder 399, better known as the Coat Hanger Asterism or Brocchi's Cluster. This startling configuration may be found by putting Altair (Alpha Aquilae) in the right lense of your binoculars and angling them directly up toward Vega (Alpha Lyrae). Depending upon the size of your binoculars, the Coat Hanger may appear in the left lense. You'll recognize it without any effort because six stars align to form the hanger and four others curve beside it, creating the hook. This neat little figure sticks up on one end and is sure to delight stargazers of all ages. Be sure to hang it in your treasure chest and point it out to your pals.

SAGITTA THE ARROW

Sagitta is one of the few constellations that actually looks like its name. Sagitta is said to be one of the arrows with which Hercules killed Aquila the Eagle that ate the liver of Prometheus who gave fire to man. Another story relates that Sagitta was used to kill Ophiuchus, the Serpent Bearer, who raised so many people from the dead such as Orion the Hunter, that Pluto, god of the underworld, complained to Jupiter that he was losing too much business!

Sagitta may also have been the arrow which Hercules shot at the Stymphalian birds, Cygnus, Aquila and the Vulture. It is also known as the arrow that Apollo used to slay the Cyclops. Others know it as an errant arrow shot by Sagittarius the Archer.

* * * * *

In binoculars Sagitta is easy to find by starting at Altair (Alpha Aquilae), the bright star in the middle of a row of three. From Altair go roughly one handspan or about a third of the distance to Vega (Alpha Lyrae) and look toward the northeast. The arrow points eastward away from the summer birds, alone without a bow. Two double stars at its western end form the feathers. Continuing eastward, the point ends at Delta Sagittae. Halfway between Delta and Gamma Sge is M71 (NGC-6838), a small faint, fuzzy globular cluster. Hardly a Moon's diameter away is Harvard 20, a sparse clutter of stars which easily fits in the same lense of your binoculars.

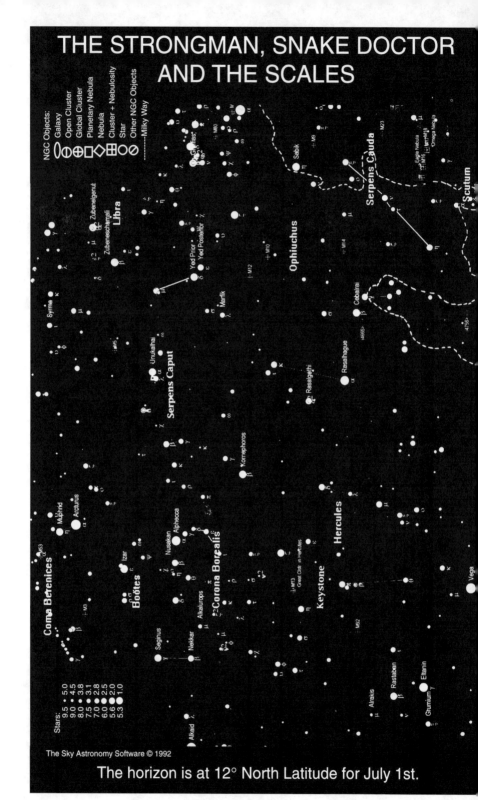

THE STRONGMAN, SNAKE DOCTOR AND THE SCALES

The Sky Astronomy Software © 1992

The horizon is at 12° North Latitude for July 1st.

HERCULES, RAMBO OF THE SKY

Hercules the Kneeling One or Strongman is the fifth largest constellation. It is an ancient star group that developed from Mesopotamian culture and may be identical to the Sumerian hero Gilgamesh. Gilgamesh, like Hercules, was half mortal and was assigned twelve superhuman labors. One of his labors is described under Hydra the Female Water Snake.

The Hercules we know today comes from the Greeks who called him Heracles. We know him as Hercules because Latin names are used for the constellations. The Romans adopted many of the Greek gods and changed their names; for instance, Zeus became Jupiter and Hera, Juno. Heracles was the result of an adventure between his father Zeus and a mortal, Alcmene. To appease his jealous wife Hera, Zeus named the child Heracles which means "Glory to Hera," but the name did not make up for his father's infidelity in Hera's eyes. She placed two serpents in the cradle to kill Heracles, but the baby "Rambo" strangled them easily.

The greatest feats of Hercules started when he killed the Nemean Lion which later became the constellation Leo. Another task was to kill Hydra, the many-headed snake and to capture alive the boar of Erymanthus of Arcadia. Nine other labors followed which were supposedly atonement for crimes Hercules committed while under a spell of madness imposed by Hera.

* * * * *

Hercules is a sprawling figure in a somewhat vacant area east of Corona Borealis, the Northern Crown, a pretty semi-circle of stars, and west of the bright star Vega (Alpha Lyrae) in Lyra the Lute or Vulture. Hercules lies upside down and resembles a spider with a large trapezoid in the center representing the body from which five legs radiate in different directions. The trapezoid is called the Keystone asterism formed by Eta Herculis, Zeta, Pi and Epsilon.

M13, the Great Hercules Cluster, which was spotted by Sir Edmond Halley a half a century before Charles Messier labeled it, resides just inside the cluster. It is one of the largest and brightest globular clusters in the northern sky and lies 2.5° south of Eta which marks the upper northern corner of the Keystone. Even though you may spot it with your naked eye on a dark night, it is a typical messy object looking like a bright smudge. But when a telescope is turned on it, M13 is a winner! M92 (NGC-6341), another globular cluster but not as large or bright as M13, is about 6° north of Pi which is the northwest corner star of the Keystone.

Rasalgethi (Alpha), meaning the "Head of Hercules," lies close to the south border of Hercules. It is a supergiant, a double varying in brightness every 90 days. Try not to confuse it with Rasalhague (Alpha Ophiuchi) which lies less than a handspan away and is the brighter of the two.

OPHIUCHUS THE SERPENT BEARER

Ophiuchus, a real tongue stumbler of a name, is derived from the Greek words "ophis" meaning "serpent" and "cheiro-o" meaning "handle." Ophiuchus is associated with Aesculapius, the son of Apollo and a mortal woman named Coronis. As a child Ophiuchus (Aesculapius) was taught the skills of medicating and healing by the wise Centaur Chiron. He also learned how to restore life to the dead when he killed a snake one day and another snake nearby rushed over with an herb in its mouth and revived it. Ophiuchus saw a good thing coming and grabbed the herb which enabled him to save countless people.

You can imagine how all this activity put quite a crimp on Pluto's business in the Realm of the Dead because nobody was dying anymore. Pluto appealed to Jupiter to stop this nonsense, so Jupiter sent Aquila the Eagle to strike Ophiuchus down with a thunderbolt. Poor Ophiuchus was done in but Jupiter placed the great doctor holding his friend, the snake, in the sky so that his wonderful knowledge would not be lost.

One of the most famous charitable acts of Ophiuchus was to make Orion the Hunter as good as new after the Scorpion stung and killed him. Ophiuchus stands over Scorpius, his feet ready to squash it after Orion is restored.

* * * * *

Lying on his side Ophiuchus sprawls just to the south of Hercules, resembling the Tin Man with his peaked hat in "Wizard of Oz." The head of Ophiuchus is Rasalhague (Alpha Ophiuchi) which forms almost a perfect triangle with Vega (Alpha Lyrae) and Altair (Alpha Aquilae). Rasalhague also forms the peak of a wide triangle with the double stars Cheleb (Beta) and Gamma making up one end and Sigma and Kappa, a second pair of doubles, the other.

Just a tad northeast of Cebairai (Beta), IC 4665, a bright open cluster nearly the width of two Moons, stands out in binoculars. About two-thirds down a line from Cheleb to Marfik (Lambda) and centrally located in the hexagonal figure of Ophiuchus is the first of three messy objects, M10 (NGC-6254), a globular cluster. In the same binocular field is M12 (NGC-6218), another fine globular cluster. The third, M14 (NGC-6402), is in the eastern portion of Ophiuchus, roughly a third of the way from Gamma near Cheleb (Beta) down to Sabik (Eta) at the doctor's right knee. Like the other clusters M14 is a fuzzy spot but stands out easily.

Grab your snorkle tube and let's dive back into the Milky Way Stream down to Theta Oph, the right foot of Ophiuchus. Here amidst the star shoals is a dark squiggle, the intriguing "S" Nebula or Barnard 72. This short, small nebula extends from the northwest part of the Pipe Nebula, an enormous dark area that covers more than 7° of southern Ophiuchus. About a finger from Barnard 72 is M19 (NGC-6273) a globular cluster and about 4.5° southwest of it on the Ophiuchus-Scorpius border is yet another, M62 (NGC-6266), a wispy blob amidst a magnificent field of stars.

SERPENS CAPUT AND SERPENS CAUDA
THE SERPENT

This is a unique constellation because it is divided into two parts, Serpens Caput the Head and Serpens Cauda the Tail. This division happened because the huge snake winds through the legs of Ophiuchus the Serpent Bearer who is holding it in both hands.

This is the serpent that presumably gave Ophiuchus the magic herb which brought people back to life. Snakes symbolize fertility, rejuvenation and rebirth because they shed their skins every year and appear to be "reborn."

*   *   *   *   *

Serpens Caput is the more conspicuous with its small belt of stars, but that's not saying much! Easier to locate is Unukalhai from the Arabic meaning the "serpent's neck" which is about one handspan and a half west of Marfik (Lambda Ophiuchi). Why do we plod through this dim constellation? So that we may find M5 (NGC-5904), one of the better globular clusters in a relatively uncluttered section. M5 sticks out as a fuzzy patch parked beside a dim star a bit more than half a handspan southwest of Unukalhai.

Now to Serpens Cauda, the tail end which Ophiuchus holds in his right hand marked by Tau and Nu Ophiuchi. About half a handspan southeast is M16 (NGC-6611), the Eagle Nebula. This open cluster spans half a degree, the diameter of the Moon. Its glow is discernible with binoculars, as is another open cluster, IC 4756, which is twice the size of M16. This is a delightfully complex area well worth scanning and the two merit gold stars in your treasure chest.

LIBRA THE SCALES

Southwest of Ophiuchus the Serpent Bearer in a relatively barren field is Libra, one of the twelve signs of the Zodiac. Libra has a confusing history and did not appear to be known among the Mediterranean peoples. Instead it represented the extended giant claws of Scorpius. Its two brightest stars, Zubeneschemali (Alpha Librae), the Northern Claw and Zubenelgenubi (Beta Lib) the Southern Claw, bear beautiful, rhymic Arabic names. But something happened that caused astronomers to snip off the claws and put Libra in their place. As a sky detective, perhaps you may figure out what it was. Here are the facts. Judge for yourself.

Some 5000 years ago the Sumerians, a prominent Mesopotamian civilization, recognized Scorpius with its enormous extended claws. But around 2000 B.C. the Chaldeans are thought to have called this area Zib-ba Anna, the "Balance of Heaven" because Libra coincided with the autumn equinox. Thus Scorpius lost its pinchers and Libra reigned in their stead.

During Caesar's time in 46 B.C. the Romans claimed that they invented Libra the Scales because the Sun appeared there at the autumnal equinox. Libra became the sign which weighed the lengths of day and night.

Who do you think was the culprit who chopped off the claws, the Chaldeans or the Romans? Probably the Romans did not really invent Libra but revived it. In any case, the Scorpion doesn't need its claws because it stings its enemies.

* * * * *

105

THE SUMMER SOUTHERN SKY

The Sky Astronomy Software © 1992

The horizon is at 12° North Latitude for July 1st.

Although Libra's stars are faint, they form a somewhat lopsided but distinctive diamond. Look for it slightly northwest of the bright arc of four stars forming the head of Scorpius.

SCORPIUS THE SCORPION

Scorpius is one of the most easily recognized constellations in the southeastern summer sky because it actually does resemble a scorpion. In the Greek story about its encounter with Orion the Hunter, the Scorpion was commanded by Gaia, the Goddess of the Earth, to sting Orion the Hunter because Orion made one brazen claim too many that he could kill any animal on Earth at his whim. Orion dies as he disappears in the west just as Scorpius rises in the southeast. But all is not lost! Ophiuchus, the Serpent Bearer cures Orion and the next evening Orion rises, renewed and vigorous again. Scorpius is trampled under Ophiuchus's feet but Ophiuchus gets it in the neck too when Jupiter, angry at him for interfering, orders Aquila the Eagle to descend upon Ophiuchus with a thunderbolt. Zap! Ophiuchus succumbs. The story does not tell you how Ophiuphus comes alive nor how Scorpius grows anew from his squashed shape, but they both make it and the whole scene is reenacted again the next evening.

The Maoris of New Zealand see Scorpius as Maui's fish hook. Maui was fishing with the hook which was once a jawbone of an ancestor when he caught it on the bottom of the sea. Lunging hard, he heaved the hook to the surface and discovered a huge fish-island impaled on it. The enormous island broke into two islands which became the North and South islands of New Zealand.

Other seafaring nations such as India carried on the sea-oriented images of Scorpius, seeing it as a Palm Tree or a Sting Ray, while inland jungle tribes of Brazil envisioned the Great Serpent as did the Chinese.

The Sumerians of Mesopotamia knew Scorpius as Gortab when its claws extended into Libra the Scales. The Chaldeans may have lopped off the claws around 2500 B.C. and put a Balance or Scale in their place. The Romans in the first century claimed the responsibility as well. Who done it? The answer is lost in the ocean of time.

* * * * *

Lying below Ophiuchus, Scorpius is a beautiful constellation rearing nearly straight up and resembling exactly what it stands for. Of the four bright stars that make up the head, Graffias or Acrab (Beta Scorpii), meaning "claws" in Latin, is a quadruple star system. Dschubba (Delta), Ti and Rho continue the shallow arc.

Twelve stars outline the body which curves down toward the southeast, ending with Shaula (Lambda) and Lesath (Nu), the Stinger. Antares (Alpha), the second star below the head, and the Scorpion's glowing orangish heart, is an enormous red supergiant. Its name is derived from the Greek words *Anti* and *Ares* meaning the "rival of" Ares or Mars, the War God, due to its similar reddish color. Antares is about 600 million miles across and some 700 times the diameter of the Sun or roughly the same size as Betelgeuse (Alpha Orionis), one of the largest stars known in our galaxy. Antares lies close to the ecliptic and is often near to and occasionally occulted or blocked out by the Moon.

One and a half degrees or a finger's width west of Antares is M4 (NGC-6121), one of the closest globular clusters to the solar system. With binoculars it appears as a misty patch with a strong suggestion of faint chains entangled within.

Scan four stars down from Antares to Zeta, which, in binoculars, shows a tight trio of stars enmeshed in a web of bluish gas. Immediately above or north of Zeta is the glowing open star cluster NGC-6231, a luminescent cocoon.

Follow the tail around to the double stars called the "Cat's Eyes" which form the Stinger; Shaula (Lambda) which in Arabic means "the sting" and Lesath (Nu). There you are in position to view two of the most stunning open clusters of the southern sky. Two fingers east of the Stinger is M7 (NGC-6475), easily visible to the naked eye as a speckled glow, but in binoculars is a glorious tangle of necklaces with the distinctive letter 'K' or 'X' embedded in it. To view it with binoculars, put the right lens on the Stinger. M7 will appear in the left lense. From this stepping stone move north up to M6 (NGC-6405), the Butterfly Cluster, a smaller and tighter knot of stars to the unaided eye, but in binoculars splays into two graceful butterfly wings adorned with tiny pearls.

One last unusual star formation may capture your eye, the Little Hockey Stick asterism. With M6 in the left lense of your binoculars, the asterism may appear in the right lense with a slight adjustment. The Little Hockey Stick is distinctive in a relatively star-free spot.

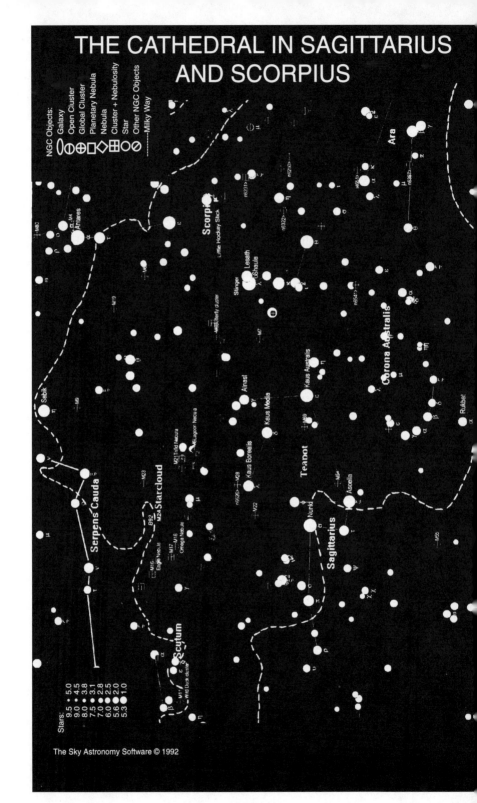

THE CATHEDRAL IN SAGITTARIUS AND SCORPIUS

The Sky Astronomy Software © 1992

SAGITTARIUS THE ARCHER AND THE TEAPOT ASTERISM

Beside the Stinger of Scorpius is the cathedral of the Milky Way Stream, its vaults ablaze with star clouds containing millions of stars. Here you face the nucleus of our galaxy, the densest, most crammed concentration of stars, nebulae and debris. Sagittarius is enveloped by these great masses that glow so brightly that you see them as white, globular clouds.

Sagittarius is pictured as a half-horse, half-man with bow drawn, its arrow pointing at Antares (Alpha Scorpii), the glowing reddish heart of the Scorpion. Greek myth says that Sagittarius shot Scorpius to avenge the death of Orion the Hunter which the Scorpion stung after Orion boasted that he could slaughter all creatures both great and small on Earth. His arrogance so angered Gaia, the Goddess of the Earth, that she punished Orion by commanding the Scorpion to kill him.

* * * * *

Only a few brilliant superstars shine through this thick maze of the Milky Way Stream. To visualize the Greek figure is a supreme test of your imagination. Instead modern stargazers use the Teapot asterism which is a simple, wide, inverted "V" formed by Ascella (Zeta Sagittarii), Phi, Lambda, Kaus Media (Delta) and Kaus Australis (Epsilon). To its east Tau and Nunki (Sigma) form the handle and to its west, Alnasl (Gamma) and Eta form the spout.

Other imaginative folks see the Milk Dipper which is formed by the stars in the handle, Nunki (Sigma), Tau, Ascella (Zeta), Phi and Lambda. The Archer's bow and arrow are also formed by the stars in the Teapot. Instead of an archer the Egyptians saw a centaur with bow and arrow drawn but his forefeet rested in Corona Australis, the constellation below Sagittarius.

It's easy to lose your way in this convoluted section of the Milky Way Stream, so try beginning at M7 (NGC-6475), the refulgent star cluster two fingers east of the Stinger in Scorpius. From this stepping stone move north up to M6 (NGC-6405), the Butterfly Cluster. Using only your naked eye scan northeast to the dark pocket above the dense star clouds and you may see an oval glow. You have arrived at M8 (NGC-6523), one of the most thrilling nebulae in the southern sky. Popularly known as the Lagoon Nebula it resembles, in binoculars, a flying saucer. In the same field just above it is another magnificent nebula, M20 (NGC-6514), the Trifid Nebula, which may resemble a glittering beatle to your imagination.

Brightest and largest of the globular clusters is M22 (NGC-6656), a little more than a fist's width away and northeast of Lambda at the top of the Teapot. In binoculars M22 is an almost perfectly round fuzz ball.

Moving back to the "black hole" where the Lagoon and Trifid Nebulae puncture its dark depths, go directly north into the glittering patch of stars which is M24, the Small Sagittarius Star Cloud. This glistening shoal resembling grainy sand stands out because it is etched by surrounding fingers of dark nebulae. One of these intruding fingers is the round hole, Barnard 92, which is on the northwest edge of the Star Cloud.

Above M24 are two more objects visible in binoculars in the same field; M18 (NGC-6613), an open star cluster and M17 (NGC-6618), the Omega Nebula named for its omega-shape.

Many other clots of stars and fantastic patterns pepper Sagittarius. Before leaving its unsurpassed complex beauty, move roughly one handspan northeasterly to another shimmering mass of stars. This is the Scutum Star Cloud and should not be overlooked.

CORONA AUSTRALIS
THE SOUTHERN CROWN

Tucked under the base of the Teapot asterism in Sagittarius is the Southern Crown, a poor cousin to the Northern Crown. The Southern Crown forms two semi-circles of faint stars with the western loop smaller and fainter.

Corona Australis is the wreath that Bacchus, the God of Wine, placed in the sky to honor his mother Semele. The result of one of Jupiter's illicit love affairs, Bacchus was snatched from the burning body of his mother who was murdered by Juno, Jupiter's jealous wife.

* * * * *

Corona Australis is home to NGC-6541, a globular cluster which is parked to the east of the star which ends the western fainter loop. Begin at Gamma Coronae Australis and follow the eastern circlet to Theta (CrA). Sweep along the fainter curve of stars where you may intersect the faint glow of the cluster just east of the end star.

To make stargazing more fun, crank up your creative talents and envision a tea setting with stars from Sagittarius, Scorpius and Corona Australis. We already see the Teapot. Augment it with a teaspoon formed by the three bright stars above and east of the Teapot which usually forms its elongated handle. Ice tea drinkers like lemon in their tea. Wouldn't Corona Australis make a fine lemon slice? What else is needed? A cup! It might be found in the curving tail of Scorpius. Use your imaginative imagery and challenge yourself!

ARA THE ALTAR

A handspan below the tail of Scorpius before it curls is Ara, adjacent to Norma the Carpenter's Square.

Ara is the altar on which Centaurus the Centaur is offering Lupus the Wolf. It may also represent the one that the gods built after they defeated the Titans. The smoke from the burning incense may represent the Milky Way that courses through the Altar.

* * * * *

The stars forming the Altar are bright enough to pick out within the Milky Way Stream. In the German depiction of the Altar, the flames from the incense rise southward whereas the Dutch Altar shows the smoke rising northward. The Greeks also saw an upside-down lighthouse, its light pointing downward.

Ara contains several clusters discernible in binoculars. I-4651, an open cluster, is one pinkie west of Alpha Arae, the first bright star encountered south of Theta Scorpii in the tail of Scorpius. NGC-6397 is a faint but busy-looking globular cluster about half a handspan southeasterly from I-4651 and slightly less than that northwest of Beta Arae.

X

The Summer Obscure Constellations

On the north the German astronomer Jakob Bartsch in 1624 created Camelopardalis the Camel to commemorate the one that brought Rebecca to Isaac. The Camel was later changed to a Giraffe because of its shape and numerous faint stars. The head and neck are thrust between Polaris and Draco with the body standing upon Auriga and Perseus. Camelopardalis contains NGC-1502, a bright open cluster, but finding it is a challenge. Try looking for a smudge about one and a half handspans east of the "W" shape of Cassiopeia.

Telescopium was invented by de Lacaille to commemorate the invention of the telescope. The Telescope is inserted below and to the west of Corona Australis, the Southern Crown. Only its two brightest stars are readily discernible in binoculars; the rest take patience to ferret out.

If your eye catches a single bright star southeast of the Telescope, its Alpha Pavonis the bright eye of Pavo the Peacock which is explored under the Autumn Section.

Your Summer Treasure Chest

DATE	TIME	LOCATION	WEATHER			OBJECT NAME
			Clouds?	Haze?	Moon Phase	And No.

Your Summer Treasure Chest

Constellation	Type of Object Clus, Gal, Neb	Binocs/eye (Type)	Description Shape, Color Brightness	Comments

XI

Autumn Sky Preview

$\mathcal{N}$o soap opera is worth its salt without a fair damsel in distress who is rescued by the hero after he challenges and kills the villain and then wins her hand at the end. The Andromeda Drama of the autumn sky screen fits the bill perfectly. Queen Cassiopeia rules in the northeast with King Cepheus looking on above her. The Princess Andromeda, chained to a rock by the sea, awaits a horrible death at the mouth of Cetus the Whale. But all is not lost for Perseus the Hero is approaching below Cassiopeia for the kill.

A great deal of swimming goes on in autumn within the Celestial Sea. The Dolphin cavorts high above Pegasus who was born from the sea among Pisces the Fishes. The Sea Goat hopes Aquarius will pour him some wine from his jug, but Aquarius seems intent on trying to drown the Southern Fish which has flipped over Grus the Crane which wades along the southern shore with three other birds.

Two extraordinary jewels stun the mind; M31, the Great Andromeda Galaxy, a glowing oval brooch of pearls on Andromeda's hip and NGC-869 and NGC-884, the Double Cluster in Perseus, twin diamond pins studding his sword.

AUTUMN SKY LOOKING NORTH

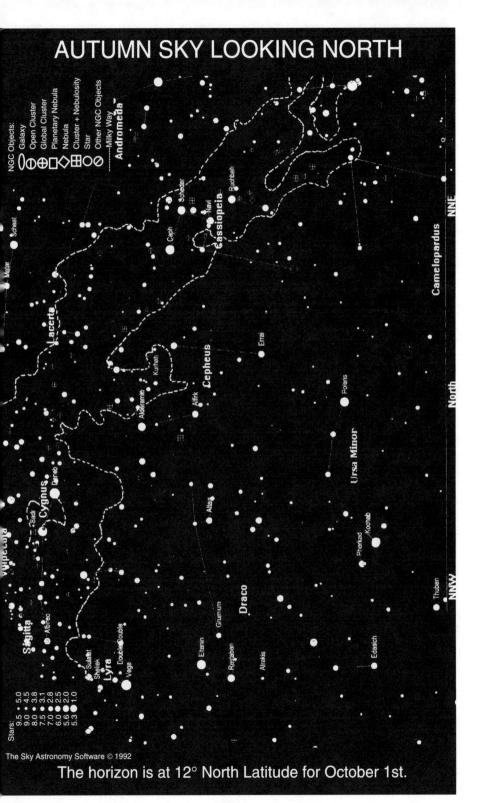

The horizon is at 12° North Latitude for October 1st.

The Sky Astronomy Software © 1992

119

AUTUMN SKY LOOKING EAST

NGC Objects:
- Galaxy
- Open Cluster
- Global Cluster
- Planetary Nebula
- Nebula
- Cluster + Nebulosity
- Star
- Other NGC Objects
- Milky Way

Stars:
9.5 • 5.0
9.0 • 4.5
8.0 • 3.8
7.5 • 3.1
7.0 • 2.8
6.0 • 2.5
5.6 • 2.0
5.3 • 1.0

Aquarius
Diphda
Cetus
Fornax
Baten Kaitos
Azha
Mira
Alrescha
Kaffaljidhma
Menkar
Pisces
Markab
Algenib
Mesarthim
Sheratan
Aries
Hamal
Scheat
Matar
Alpheratz
Andromeda
Mirach
Triangulum
Sterope
Maia
Electra Taygeta
Alcyone
Atlas
Merope
Pleiades
Almach
Atik
Menkib
Algol

The Sky Astronomy Software © 1992

The horizon is at 12° North Latitude for October 1st.

AUTUMN SKY LOOKING SOUTH

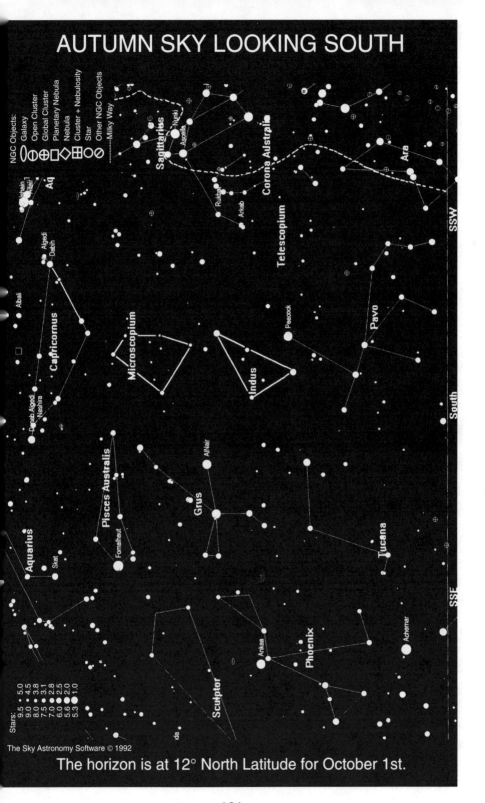

NGC Objects:

- Galaxy
- Open Cluster
- Global Cluster
- Planetary Nebula
- Nebula
- Cluster + Nebulosity
- Star
- Other NGC Objects
- Milky Way

Stars:
- 9.5 = 5.0
- 9.0 = 4.5
- 8.0 = 3.8
- 7.5 = 3.1
- 7.0 = 2.8
- 6.0 = 2.5
- 5.6 = 2.0
- 5.3 = 1.0

The Sky Astronomy Software © 1992

The horizon is at 12° North Latitude for October 1st.

AUTUMN SKY LOOKING WEST

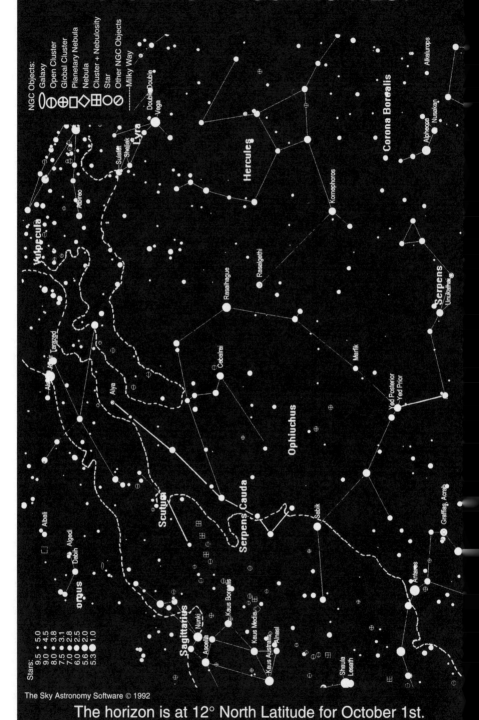

The horizon is at 12° North Latitude for October 1st.

The Sky Astronomy Software © 1992

122

THE ANDROMEDA DRAMA

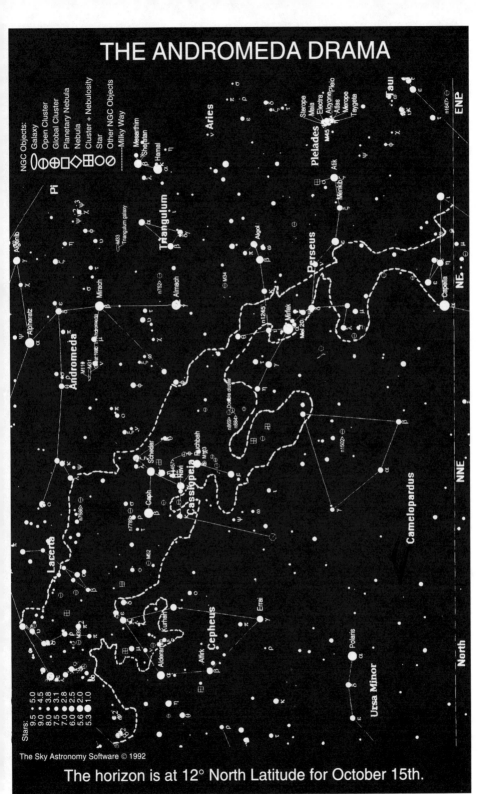

The Sky Astronomy Software © 1992

The horizon is at 12° North Latitude for October 15th.

CASSIOPEIA THE QUEEN

In the northeast Cassiopeia, the Queen of Ethiopia, sits on her throne. She is the crooked "M" of five stars that rises on its side.

The Andromeda Drama begins when Cassiopeia, a very beautiful but vain and boostful queen, brags that she is even fairer than the loveliest of all the sea nymphs, the Nereids. The girls get together and complain to Dad, Poseidon, God of the Sea. To punish Cassiopeia Poseidon condemns her to forever sit upon her throne. Worse yet, Poseidon sends a horrible, slobbering sea monster, Cetus the Whale, to ambush the Ethiopians and if they go to sea, to devour them.

King Cepheus asks what he must do to save his people and free his wife from her bondage. He is told to chain his lovely teenaged daughter Andromeda to a rock where she will be torn to pieces and eaten by the monster. Obeying Poseidon's command, he binds Andromeda by the shore and with great despair, stands nearby to await her death.

Fortunately for them all, Perseus the Hero happens to be zooming along on his hang-glider which he has exchanged for the winged sandals Minerva gave him and notices all the commotion. The next episode of this soap opera is told under Perseus.

* * * * *

Cassiopeia is sometimes referred to as the Broken Back Chair probably because it forms a zigzag. Modern stargazers may see it as a reclining chair or even better, the "Golden Arches." Some Arab peoples saw Cassiopeia together with Perseus who rises below her as the Tinted Hand. This may represent the practice of Arab women who painted their hands and feet with henna, a reddish dye as a prevention for sunburn. Caph (Beta Cassiopeias) means "Dyed Hand" in Arabic.

Because the Milky Way Stream flows through Cassiopeia, the constellation is sprinkled with star clusters. Lying

124

about half a handspan above Caph (Beta) is M52 (NGC-7654). Taking a line from Schedar (Alpha) through Beta and extending it an equal distance will almost intersect M52, a faint glow. Three degrees southwest of Schedar (Alpha) is NGC-7789, another but much larger cluster. On the opposite side of Schedar is NGC-103, another smudge.

Brightest and best of them all is NGC-457 located about two degrees south-southwest of Ruchbah (Delta Cass), the fourth star down from Caph (Beta). The brightest stars appear to form an owl with two bright stars forming the eyes, hence the name the Owl Cluster or E.T. Peruse down through the rest of Cassiopeia and discover many beautiful star patterns.

CEPHEUS THE KING

Cepheus lies to the west of his queen outside the Milky Way Stream. A line extended through Schedar (Alpha Cassiopeiae) and Caph (Beta Cass) brings you into Cepheus which looks like an upside down square house with a steep-peaked roof marked by Errai (Gamma Cephei) which points to Polaris the North Star (Alpha Ursae Minoris). Cepheus has the unhappy role in the Andromeda Drama of chaining Andromeda, his beautiful daughter, to a rock by the shore where Cetus the Whale, actually a grotesque monster, will devour her.

* * * * *

The most noticeable object in Cepheus may be Mu Cephei the Garnet Star. Mu Cep is an obese red giant and is the reddest star visible to your naked eye. It varies not only in brightness but also in color. Some have deemed it ruddy, others golden yellow. Decide the color for yourself when you find Mu just southwest of a line drawn between Alderamin (Alpha Cephei) and Delta Cep which form the base of the house.

Delta itself is a special star in that it is classified as the prototype Cepheid variable. Its regular variations in light within a certain period has served as a yardstick for determining distances between the stars and other objects.

PERSEUS THE HERO

Perseus rides on his hang-glider, his peaked helmet jutting toward Cassiopeia above him. As related in Cassiopeia, Perseus happens to see the very attractive Andromeda in dire straits, looks over the situation and decides there must be something in it for him besides the girl. He's well equipped for the rescue as he not only carries an enormous sword and specially polished shield, but also the severed head of Medusa, the queen of the terrible Gorgons. During his previous, adventure he killed Medusa by watching her reflection on the shield.

Perseus strikes an agreement with Cepheus that if he kills the monster Cetus and rescues Andromeda, he wins her and half of the kingdom. When the great slobbering monster appears, our Hero cautions Andromeda to keep her eyes closed and not peek while he pops the snake-head of Medusa from his Walmart shopping bag. Cetus turns into a huge rock, Perseus gets the girl and everybody lives happily ever after.

* * * * *

Our Hero lounges about a handspan from Epsilon Cassiopeiae, the lower of the five stars forming the "M". Sight along a line from Navi (Gamma Cass) through Ruchbah (Delta Cass) which intersects Mirfak (Alpha Persei), the Elbow. Two graceful arcs of stars curve outward from Mirfak, one toward the southeast and the other eastward toward the Pleiades Cluster. The short arm extending southward about two-thirds of a handspan from Mirfak contains Algol (Beta) the Demon star, known as the winking or evil eye of Medusa. Algol does blink in a fashion because its companion star eclipses it for about ten hours. The brightening and dimming process takes approximately 69 hours and is an interesting phenomenon to monitor.

The most famous clusters of the autumn sky are NGC-869 and NGC-884 known as the Double Cluster. So bright are these two open star colonies that your naked eye picks them out easily as a beautiful glow between Cassiopeia and Perseus. The clusters appear to lie side by side but are actually just in line from our vantage point. They have been recorded by the Chinese at least since 2585 B.C. Besides finding a spot for them in your treasure chest, check out the surrounding area which has images galore! Don't miss the large chain of stars that loops down from the Double Cluster.

Have you encountered Mel 20, the little dragon or "S" yet? It curls under Mirfak (Alpha Persei) and is one of the prettiest sights in the region. Only two fingers southeast of the little dragon is the open cluster NGC-1245 looking like a little puff of smoke from its mouth.

About two-thirds of a handspan further southeast is M34 (NGC-1039), a bright knot immersed in nebulosity and a treasure worth logging. Another way to find M34 is to go up about three fingers west-northwest from Algol (Beta Per).

The Perseids, one of the best meteor showers, occurs every year between August 10 and 14. Refer to Appendix III for details.

ANDROMEDA THE CHAINED PRINCESS

Andromeda, the lovely daughter of Cassiopeia and Cepheus, is understandably terrified at the prospect of becoming the meal of Cetus the Whale. Perseus, that enterprising lad zipping along on his hang-glider at just the right moment, rescues her by pulling out the severed head of

127

Perseus Rescues Andromeda fron Cetus the Sea Monster

Medusa from his Walmart bag which turns the monster into stone. Back into the bag goes the head, the Hero claims the maiden and everybody is happy!

* * * * *

The only sad part about Andromeda is that she has to share the star Alpheratz (Alpha Andromedae) which marks her head, with another constellation, Pegasus the Flying Horse. Alpheratz (Alpha) which means "Navel of the Horse" forms the northeast corner of the Great Square of Pegasus. A line drawn through Epsilon and Ruchbah (Delta Cassiopeiae) points to Alpheratz.

Andromeda is the home of M31 (NGC-224), the magnificent Great Andromeda Galaxy, thought to be 2,400,000 light years from Earth. It is an extraordinary whirlpool of light and is the most distant object that your naked eye can detect. A spiral galaxy like our own Milky Way, M31 is at least twice its size and populated by over 400 billion stars. It has been known as the Little Cloud as far back as A.D. 905 and is possibly the largest of the Local Group of galaxies of which ours is a member.

To locate M31 start at Alpheratz (Alpha Andromedae) and hop northeasterly down through Pi and Mu. Turn left or northwest about a finger from Mu to the dim star Nu. About one pinkie east or above Nu is M31 which resembles an elongated, luminous football. Another way to find M31 is to make a "V" of Caph (Beta Cassiopeiae), Schedar (Alpha Cass) and Navi (Delta Cass) and extend it to Mirach (Beta And), the first bright star you see. From Mirach hop one finger northeast to Mu and another finger in the same direction to Nu which is just below the galaxy. If you have trouble finding it, rotate your binoculars around gently which may make it easier to capture M31's oval glow.

NGC-752, a large open cluster the size of 11 Moon diameters, is well worth a gander. From Mirach (Beta And) charge down to Almach (Gamma And) which marks Andromeda's foot. NGC-752's loosely gathered stars are about one handspan south and slightly west of Almach.

TRIANGULUM THE TRIANGLE

The Triangle is sandwiched between Andromeda and Aries the Ram. If it wasn't for M33 (NGC-598), one of the three great spirals in the Local Group ot galaxies, the Triangle would be relegated to the Obscure Constellations section. Although M33 is the closest face-on galaxy and its magnitude is within the limits of your naked eye, it is a challenge to spot. In binoculars it is a misty cloud best found by sighting on a line southeasterly from M31, the Andromeda Galaxy, to Mirach (Beta Andromedae) and extending it about the same distance. M33 is at least double the size of M31 and much dimmer. A very dark sky is essential to see this faint powderpuff.

PEGASUS THE WINGED HORSE AND THE GREAT SQUARE ASTERISM

Prominent in the eastern autumn sky is the Great Square of Pegasus, the Winged Horse, a magical beast which springs forth from the Celestial Sea. In Greek legends his first touchdown on Earth is upon the summit of Mt Helicon and from his hooves a miraculous fountain gushes forth.

Pegasus is the beautiful snow-white steed of the hero Bellerophon, the prince of Corinth. Like Hercules, he is belabored with impossible deeds. He manages to accomplish them mostly because of the strength, deftness and loyalty of his winged mount. When Bellerophon becomes brash from all of his successes and demands a seat among the gods, Jupiter knocks him off the back of Pegasus with a thunderbolt and Bellerophon crashes to the ground. Another version relates that Jupiter sends a fly to sting Pegasus, which makes it rear without warning, bucking Bellerophon off.

* * * * *

The Square covers an area in which two of your hands held together fit inside. The Hindus saw the Square as a bedstead that represented the 26th and 27th lunar station that provided a proper resting place for the swiftly moving Moon. The Arawaks in South America pictured a huge barbecue grill, while the Egyptians considered Pegasus as the sky emblem of a ship. The Phoenicians, in a similar frame of mind, thought of the entirety of Pegasus as the figurehead of a ship.

Today's stargazers might think of the Square which is slightly canted as the Baseball Diamond. Fire up your imagination and look for the ten-star team getting ready to field a short hitter. Start first at Algenib (Gamma Pegasi) at home base. Move to Markab (Alpha Peg) and you'll see a fielder and umpire behind it. Second base is Scheat (Beta Peg) with two stars, the pitcher and the manager nearby. Between Markap (Alpha) and Scheat (Beta) are two right fielders. The left fielder has moved behind Scheat. Alpheratz or Sirrah, which means Navel of the Horse, is third base. More umpires are visible within the Square, which may give your eyesight a test as some thirty stars may be seen without aid.

M15 (NGC-7078) is the only globular cluster in Pegasus readily seen. Lying approximately four degrees northwest of Enif (Epsilon Pegasi) the "Nose," which marks the end of the long string of stars forming the neck, M15 is a fuzzy, messy object in binoculars. M15 is unusual in that it emits strong X-ray signals, a probably indicator of a monstrous black hole.

LACERTA THE LIZARD

Lacerta, a modern constellation, was first formed by Johannes Hevelius, the Polish astronomer, except that it first resembled an animal similar to a weasel. Several other astronomers envisioned it in other forms, but the Lizard prevailed and remains as one of the prettiest squiggles in the sky.

* * * * *

Lacerta looks just like its name suggests and squirms in the Milky Way Stream. Its eight brightest stars make a faint but distinctive jiggle. A line drawn diagonally across the house in Cepheus from Alfirk (Beta Cephei) through Zeta extends to the Lizard's head.

Two open star clusters, NGC-7243 and NGC-7209, are about two pinkies apart and less than a pinkie west of Lacerta's body. NGC-7209 is a Full Moon's width and easy to spy in binoculars which also shows NGC-7243 in the same field as a slightly smaller but a tad brighter fuzzy patch.

THE CELESTIAL SEA

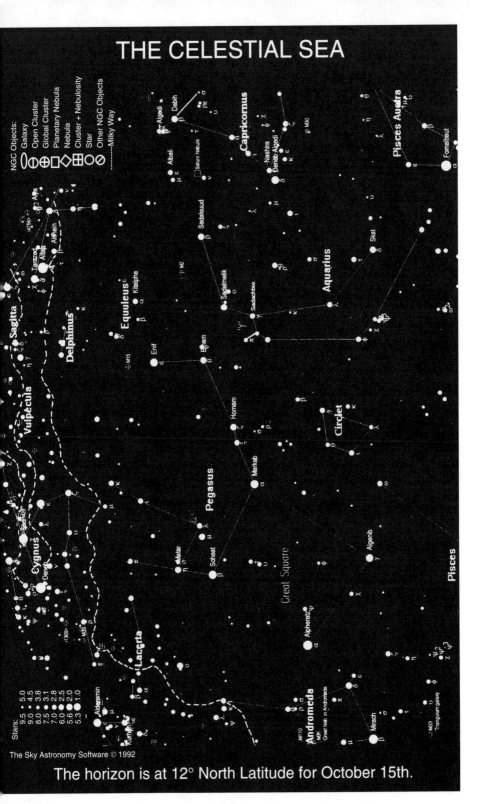

The Sky Astronomy Software © 1992

The horizon is at 12° North Latitude for October 15th.

DELPHINUS THE DOLPHIN

Cavorting all by itself outside the Milky Way Stream on its eastern bank is the little Dolphin, Delphinus. The Dolphin is the one described in Jimmy Buffett's song, "The Dolphin and the Jolly Man."

The Jolly Man was a wonderful harp player named Arion who lived in Corinth in 600 B.C. Arion played and sang so sweetly that he charmed the gods and even all the fishes in the sea. After many years he became homesick and asked the king if he could sail home for a visit. His wish was granted and a week out at sea, the ship's crew plotted to throw Arion overboard and steal his gold. Arion asked them to let him play one more song and when he did, the music was so lovely that it attracted a school of dolphins. Arion plunged into the ocean and Delphinus lifted Arion upon his back and took him to Corinth where it set the singer gently ashore.

When the ship returned with its murderous crew, the sailors were thrown into prison. Arion had a little bronze statue made of the Dolphin which he placed in the temple honoring Apollo. This pleased Apollo so much that he honored the Dolphin by putting it among the stars so that all mankind could admire it forever.

* * * * *

Although not a bright constellation, Delphinus swims alone in a sparse, dark part of the western end of the Celestial Sea about a handspan southeast of Altair (Alpha Aquilae) in the Eagle. Its four brightest stars form a distinctive diamond or parallelogram while the fifth makes up the tail. The Arabs saw the figure as a camel, others, a predatory fish or seal. The English call it Job's Coffin, the Northern Australian islanders, a trumpet shell. The Chinese had the unique idea of Delphinus as the Good Gourd and the Rotten or Frozen Gourd which are part of the third house of the Black Tortoise of Winter.

Arion (or is it Jimmy Buffett?)
Escapes on Delphinus the Dolphin

Three of the stars in the Dolphin's body are doubles; Gamma at the nose, Alpha at the back and Beta toward the tail.

PISCES THE FISHES

Swimming quietly in the Celestial Sea below Andromeda and Pegasus is the faint, spread-out constellation representing two fishes tied together with a V-shaped cord. Why they are tethered is a mystery but the idea seems to have come from the Babylonians.

According to Roman legend, the fishes were Venus and her son Cupid who were attacked by the fearful monster Typhon whom we will meet again in Capricornus. There was no way to escape Typhon except by water, so the two dove in. Venus and Cupid were changed into fishes and to keep from being separated, they tied themselves together with a string. There is some confusion with this story, however, because according to others, the larger fish was the monster in the Andromeda drama. In most myths that we read today, the monster about to attack Andromeda is Cetus the Whale.

The Chinese saw the stars that represent the line joining the fishes as a fence which they called the "Outer Enclosure." This fence is supposed to prevent the farmer from falling into the marshes. The pigs in the marshes represent the stars in Cetus the Sea Monster, which are unable to get out.

* * * * *

Even though Pisces is dim, it is a notable constellation because it contains the point at which the Sun crosses the celestial equator into the northern hemisphere each year. This point which was called the First Point of Aries because it originally lay in Aries, is the vernal equinox.

Because of precession, the slow wobble of the Earth on its axis, this point has moved into Pisces.

Enjoy fishing for Pisces by first going to the Great Square of Pegasus. About a handspan from the south side of the Square is the Circlet, an irregular diamond of six stars which marks the larger fish. A long line of faint stars trickles past the Square down to Alrischa (Alpha Piscium) which means "the Cord." From Alrischa there is another faint line which ends beside Andromeda near Mirach (Beta Andromedae). It ends at a tiny triangle, the second fish, which swims immediately above the faintly glowing spiral galaxy, M33.

Although Pisces does not contain any messy objects bright enough to be seen in binoculars, it is an important constellation not only because the vernal equinox occurs there but also because a triple conjunction of Jupiter, Saturn and some stars occurred in 7 B.C. This conjunction is considered by some to be the Star of Bethlehem.

AQUARIUS THE WATER BEARER AND THE WINE GLASS ASTERISM

Straddling the central part of the Celestial Sea south of the Great Square of Pegasus and west of Cetus the Whale, Aquarius appears to be nearly hidden in its watery depths. Appropriately, Aquarius has been associated with water since the early Babylonian era. It is the "Seat of the Flowing Waters," a rainbringer which causes the annual flooding of such rivers as the Nile. Almost all cultures have the ancient story of the great flood which Aquarius represents.

In modern times Aquarius is usually associated with Ganymede, the beautiful young boy who is abducted by Jupiter to serve as a cupbearer of the gods. Ganymede was carried up to the realm of the gods by Aquila the Eagle and attended to the needs of the gods but he was mostly a glorified waiter. Ganymede is usually drawn as holding an urn from which a stream of water and nectar pours. This stream is shown by a cascade of many dim stars which flow southwesterly down to Fomalhaut, the bright star marking the mouth of Piscis Austrinis, the Southern Fish.

The idea of luck associated with the abundance of fresh, clean water is evident in the names of three of the brightest stars in Aquarius which all begin with the Arabic word "sad," meaning luck. Sadalmelik (Alpha Aquarii) means "lucky star of the king." Sadalsuud (Beta Aqr) is "luckiest of the lucky" and Sadalakbiya or Sadachbia (Gamma Aqr) is "lucky stars of the tents."

Four stars form the Wine Glass or "Y" asterism which is the easiest part of Aquarius to locate. Using Scheat (Beta Pegasi) and Markab (Alpha Peg) which form the upper western side of the Great Square of Pegasus, draw a line through them toward the south about one and a half handspans which will intersect the tiny foursome forming the Wine Glass. The Wine Glass is so symmetrical that it looks almost the same right side up or down.

Aquarius contains M2 (NGC-7089), a compact globular cluster six degrees or one handspan north of Sadalsuud (Beta Aquarii) and nine degrees west of Sadalmelik (Alpha Aqu). In binoculars M2 is a bright oval blob easily discernible from stars.

Several meteor showers radiate from Aquarius. Consult Appendix III for detailed information.

CAPRICORNUS THE SEA GOAT

Capricornus is an ancient constellation and probably originated from the Sumerians and Babylonians who called it Suhuermashha, the goat fish. The Greeks identified it as Pan, god of the countryside, who has the horns and legs of a goat. Pan was a happy-go-lucky, harmless but mischievous little goat. He spent most of his time chasing sea sprites or sleeping it off. Occasionally this impish little fellow put people into a panic when he consumed too much demon rum and charged after them. Supposedly the word "panic" was derived from this story.

One day Pan was happily playing his pipes for his friends on the beach when Typhon, a horrible demon and his ruthless gang attacked them. Being a clever old goat, Pan jumped into the sea to turn himself into a fish and swim quickly away. Unfortunately the water was too shallow and only Pan's behind changed into the tail and fins of a fish. Just as he was swimming away from the shore, Jupiter bellowed for help. In his haste to help Jupiter, Pan forgot the right words to change himself back into a goat. He rescued Jupiter in this state and Jupiter was so grateful that he eternalized Pan in the stars just as he was — half-goat, half-fish.

* * * * *

Capricornus is a large dim constellation which may best be visualized as a boat with high, pointed bow and stern. it also resembles a boomerang or a bikini bottom. If you imagine it as a boat, you see the bow rising first with Algedi (Alpha Capricorni), a double double star and Dabih (Beta Cap). Below them a trio of dim stars continues the V-shaped line of the hull which sweeps up to the pointed stern. The stern is etched by Deneb Algedi (Delta Cap) and Nashira (Gamma Cap) which form an almost duplicate pattern of the bow. Deneb Algedi (Delta) which means "tail of the goat," is the star near which two astronomers discovered simultaneously the planet Neptune in 1846.

Capricornus is in a rather vacant area of the Celestial Sea between Aquarius and Sagittarius. Its bow points toward Aquila the Eagle, its stern toward Aquarius. In the southeastern part lies M30 (NGC-7099), one of the best although small globular clusters of the autumn sky. Outside the southeast side of the boat M30, in binoculars, shows as a round fuzzy patch less than one pinkie west of the bright star 41 Capricorni.

NGC Objects:
Galaxy
Open Cluster
Global Cluster
Planetary Nebula
Nebula
Cluster + Nebulosity
Star
Other NGC Objects
------- Milky Way

Stars:
9.5 : 5.0
9.0 : 4.5
8.0 : 3.8
7.5 : 3.1
7.0 : 2.8
6.0 : 2.5
5.6 : 2.0
5.3 : 1.0

The Sky Astronomy Software © 1992

The horizon is at 12° North Latitude for October 15th.

140

CETUS THE WHALE OR SEA MONSTER

Lurking in the depths of the Celestial Sea is the slimy, smelly sea monster Cetus. Although Cetus means "whale," it was visualized as a bizarre-looking creature whose upper body was adapted to the land and its rear like a serpent with fins.

Cetus is the villain of the Andromeda drama which would have devoured dear little Andromeda had not Perseus the Hero come along, made a deal with her parents and turned Cetus to stone with the head of Medusa that Perseus pulled out of his Walmart bag. In another version Perseus stabs the monster to death with his mighty sword.

In myths of other cultures Cetus is the evil dragon who usually abducts a beautiful maiden who is rescued by the handsome knight or giant. Some of the northern Brazilian Indian tribes pictured Cetus as a jaguar which personified the God of Violent Storms and Hurricanes.

* * * * *

Cetus, the fourth largest constellation, sprawls below Pisces in the south. Only two of its stars are bright enough to be seen without much difficulty; Menkar (Alpha Ceti) the brightest which is at the northeast side of the Circlet of five stars which forms the head and Diphda or Deneb Kaitos (Beta Ceti) at the end of a large triangle which forms its tail. The Circlet is east of Aries the Ram and west of the Pleiades star cluster. Diphda (Beta) is found by drawing a line from the eastern or lower corner stars, Alpheratz (Alpha Andromedae) and Algenib (Gamma Pegasi) of the Great Square of Pegasus.

Cetus contains Mira, an astounding variable star called the "Wonderful" or "Amazing Star" which brightens to its maximum about every 332 days. It is an obese red supergiant which is invisible for about five months and gradually builds in the next six months to its peak brillance of about second magnitude for a period of two weeks. Its change in brightness was thought to represent the beating of the heart of Cetus.

PISCIS AUSTRINUS
THE SOUTHERN FISH

The Southern Fish, a faint constellation with one bright star, Fomalhaut (Alpha Piscis Austrini) swims south of Aquarius the Water Bearer, gulping down the stream of water pouring from his jug. In stories of the great deluge, the Southern Fish's large mouth symbolizes the saving of the world because it drinks up all the water. It has also seen as the parent of Pisces the Fishes in the north.

This talented fish also proved to be a clever one in the story of Orion as the Egyptian Osiris. Osiris is murdered by Set, his brother, who cuts his body into pieces and throws it into the river Nile. Isis, Osiris's sister-wife, manages to find all the pieces of her husband's body except for the phallus. She was defeated by Piscis Austrinus who had earlier been looking for a meal. Coming upon the phallus, the Fish swallowed it. Isis couldn't get it back so she fashioned a wooden replica so that Osiris could be buried whole.

* * * * *

The key to finding the Southern Fish is the Great Square of Pegasus. Using the same line as you did to locate Aquarius, sight through Scheat (Beta Pegasi) and Markab (Alpha Peg), the western or upper corner stars of the Square south to Fomalhaut (Alpha Piscis Austrini). The Southern Fish is sometimes drawn with its back towards the north or occasionally to the south. Its fat mouth resembles that of a bass or grouper with its body extending westward about one handspan long and a half handspan wide.

Fomalhaut (Alpha Piscis Austrini) is the only bright star high in the southern sky in the early autumn evening.

142

Its name is taken from the Arabic name "Fum al Hut" meaning "fish's mouth." The Arabs also referred to it as "the Large Southern Fish" and as "the Solitary One," although Alphard (Alpha Hydrae) in Hydra the Female Water Snake also bears this title.

To the Persians Fomalhaut (Alpha Piscis Aus) was one of the four Royal Stars of Heaven. The others were Aldebaran (Alpha Tauri), Antares (Alpha Scorpii) and Regulus (Alpha Leonis).

ARIES THE RAM

Tucked between Triangulum, Pisces and Cetus is Aries the Ram. Although the Ram does not stand out, you may pick out its three brightest stars with ease. It may seem strange to find a Ram in the depths of the Celestial Sea, but the Ram was an important figure to many different cultures. Besides being the animal most frequently sacrificed to the gods, it often was considered to be Jupiter. In ancient Egypt the Ram was Ammon Ra who was the God of Fertility and Creative Life and was drawn as a man with a Ram's head. This particular Ram was special because since it was an important god, it had golden fleece. These priceless curls were the reason why Jason and his crew on the ship Argo went to so much trouble to obtain.

The story of the horrible demon-monster Typhon attacking the gods is also associated with the Ram. The Olympic gods tended to change into animals to save themselves and Jupiter became a ram and outfoxed Typhon. Jupiter was so proud of his deceit that he placed the Ram in the sky as a tribute to his own cleverness.

The Greek myth of the two children Phrixos and Helle who must flee their wicked stepmother to keep from being executed illustrates the special magic of the golden Ram. Nephele, their mother who resided in Olympus, whispered to them to jump onto the back of the Ram which appeared from Heaven beside them. They were to hang on tight and never look down as the Ram "flew" away. The kids thought it was a great ride but Helle forgot her mother's instructions and when she looked down, she slipped off and plunged into the sea. Her landing place became known as the Hellespont. Phrixos made it without mishap to Colchis which was ruled by King Aeetes. Phrixos sacrificed the Ram to Jupiter and gave its golden fleece to Aeetes who placed it in a tree which was guarded by a dragon whose eyes never closed. Jupiter honored the Ram by putting it among the stars.

The heroic Ram figures in yet another famous story, the adventures of Odysseus, King of Ithaca, in Book IX of Homer's *Odyssey*. Odysseus and his men are captured on an island inhabited by the Cyclops, a race of one-eyed giants. Imprisoned in the cave of Polyphemus, one of the Cyclops, the men are unable to escape and are eaten, one by one each night. In desperation Odysseus manages to put the Cyclops' eye out with a stake after getting the giant drunk from the ship's wine. The next morning Odysseus ties himself and each man under the belly of the Rams that Polyphemus keeps in the cave. As each Ram is turned out of the cave, Polyphemus runs his hands over their backs and does not detect the men. Odysseus and his crew escape from the island and eventually return home.

* * * * *

Aries would be a candidate for the Obscure Constellations section if it had not been the background constellation of the vernal equinox between 1730 B.C. and A.D. 420. This point at which the Sun crosses the celestial equator from north to south is not stationary due to the precession of the equinoxes. But during that time the Zodiac started there and the location became known as the First Point of Aries. The vernal equinox has moved some 30 degrees since then and is currently residing in Pisces the Fishes. It will return to Aries in the year A.D. 24,100.

Hamal (Alpha Arietis) marks the head of the Ram with two stars, Sheratan (Beta Ari) and Mesarthim (Gamma Ari) about four degrees southeast of Hamal. Mesarthim (Gamma) is a double of similar magnitude.

The Epsilon Arietid meteor shower occurs from October 12–23. Details may be found in Appendix III.

THE AUTUMN BIRDS AND THE SOUTHERN SKY

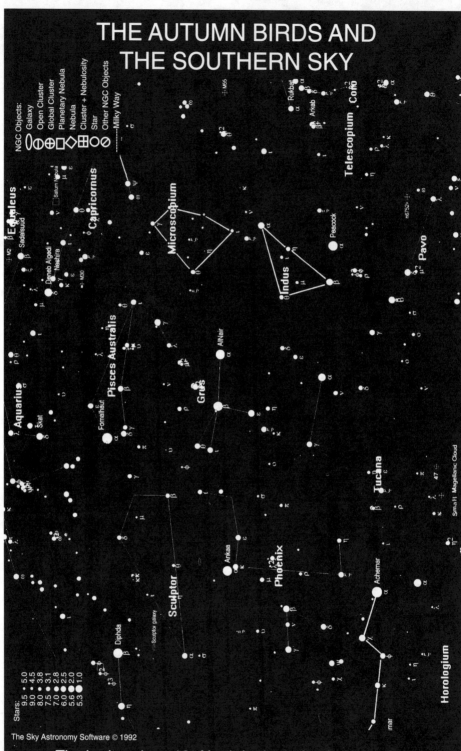

The Sky Astronomy Software © 1992

The horizon is at 12° North Latitude for October 15th.

PHOENIX

Of the twelve constellations that Pieter Dirkszoor Keyser and Friderick de Houtman introduced at the beginning of the seventeenth century, five of them are birds. Starting with Phoenix, the easternmost bird which rises from the sea haze of the southern horizon, its wings are outlined by two triangles, its neck outstretched to end at Alpha Phoenicis.

Phoenix was an amazing bird which could live for 500 years. When the Sun's rays caused its nest to burst into flames, the Phoenix perished. A startling thing happened when a wee worm crawled from the ashes. It was transformed into a new Phoenix. The new bird then carried the remains of its former self to the Sun as an offering of obedience.

* * * * *

Many civilizations imagined Phoenix as some sort of bird such as an ostrich or eagle. In China it is the Fire Bird. The Arabs also saw a primitive boat outlined in some of the stars of Phoenix. They named its brightest star Al Nair (Alpha Phoenicis), meaning "the Bright One" which they also gave to Alpha Gruis in Grus the Crane. This name has now been changed to Ankaa (Alpha Phoenicis).

GRUS THE CRANE

Immediately west of Phoenix and just below the Southern Fish is Grus whose extended neck and wings form a distinctive "X" shaped figure. Grus was also identified as the Stork of Heaven or Flamingo. Fishermen of the Marshall Islands in the western Pacific Ocean imagined its long neck as a fishing rod.

As mentioned under Phoenix, the brightest star in Grus bears the name Al Nair (Alpha Gruis) meaning "the

Bright One." At one time it was associated with Piscis Austrinis, the Southern Fish.

TUCANA THE TOUCAN

Directly below Phoenix and Grus is Toucan which is simply drawn as a rather fat triangle. In England the bird is called the Brazilian Pye. It is also known as the American Gans which means goose in Dutch.

* * * * *

Toucan would easily be a candidate for the Obscure Constellation section except for its two extraordinary features, the Small Magellanic Cloud (SMC) upon which it perches and the globular cluster, 47 Tucanae. The Small Magellanic Cloud is a satellite galaxy about 196,000 light years from Earth. It and its companion galaxy, the Large Magellanic Cloud, were seen by Ferdinand Magellan, the Portugeuse navigator, during his voyage around the world. Both galaxies appear to be interconnected.

47 Tucanae lies just east of the SMC and is second only to Omega Centauri in Centaurus as the brightest globular cluster in the sky.

PAVO THE PEACOCK

The last of the southern horizon birds rears its head west of Grus the Crane, its beady eye seemingly fixed upon Indus the Indian inserted between it and Grus. The Peacock was the royal bird long before the constellation was formed. The Greek story about the Peacock involves Juno, the jealous wife of Jupiter and Io, one of his girl friends with whom he had an affair. To save the girl from Juno's wrath, Jupiter changed Io into a white heifer. Juno, however, was wise to his old tricks and commanded Argus, a demon with one hundred eyes, to guard the heifer so that she could not escape. Jupiter conned Mercury into hypnotizing Argus but it took a long time for all of those hundred eyes to close. Argus finally fell asleep, Io escaped and Mercury killed Argus. Juno honored Argus by placing all of his eyes in the tail feathers of her favorite bird, the Peacock.

* * * * *

Pavo struts on the shore of the southern sky, its eye, Peacock (Alpha Pavonis) the only bright star in the vicinity. The Peacock's impressive tail feathers jut between Telescopium and Ara the Altar with a dozen faint stars which emulate the eyes of Argus.

Roughly one handspan southwest of Peacock (Alpha Pavonis) is NGC-6752, a bright globular cluster in binoculars showing a suggestion of necklaces entwined.

XII

The Autumn Obscure Constellations

*N*icolas Louis de Lacaille inserted Sculptor, a small faint constellation east of Fomalhaut (Alpha Piscis Austrini) and between Cetus to the north and Phoenix to the south. It is insignificant except for its vivid ruby, a variable star labeled R, which seesaws between naked-eye visibility and binocular vision in a period of 207 days.

Lacaille would not have neglected to honor two of the most important ocular instruments, the Microscope and the Telescope, which he placed in the southern sky. Separated by Indus the Indian and a vacant space, Microscopium is west of the boundary between Piscis Austrinus and Grus and north of Indus. Telescopium lies west of Indus and between Corona Australis, the Southern Crown and Ara the Altar.

Lacaille filled up the last of the space near the South Celestial Pole with one more instrument, the Octant. The Octant was the forerunner of the sextant. The constellation's only claim to fame is Alpha Octantis, the Southern Pole Star.

Indus is one of Johannes Bayer's creations, invented to possibly honor the American Indians or those of southern South America. Barely discernible, Indus mimics the stealthy, skilled Indian hunter, so masterful at tracking and catching his prey. In this case Indus might be creeping up to Pavo the Peacock who struts seemingly unaware only a few degrees to the southwest. This is only conjecture because Pavo's eye, Peacock (Alpha Pavonis) appears to stare fixedly at him.

Hydrus, the Male Water Snake, another invention of Bayer's, sticks his tail close to Achernar (Alpha Eridani), the end of Eridanus. It snakes its way between Horologium and Reticulum to the east and Tucana to the west. The Chinese also saw a serpent in Hydrus but arranged it differently. Supposedly, Hydrus is the mate of Hydra and was somehow separated from it.

Equuleus the Little Horse or Colt is so inconspicuous that few know that it is there. And no wonder, for it is just a tiny trapezoid of four faint stars inserted between the nose of Pegasus the Winged Horse and Delphinus the Dolphin. Its origin is attributed to the Greek philosopher Hipparchus. The Arabs labeled it the "First Horse" since it rose before Pegasus.

Your Autumn Treasure Chest

DATE	TIME	LOCATION	WEATHER		OBJECT NAME
			Clouds? Haze?	Moon Phase	And No.

Your Autumn Treasure Chest

Constellation	Type of Object Clus, Gal, Neb	Binocs/eye (Type)	Description Shape, Color Brightness	Comments

Appendix I

The Eighty-Eight Constellations in Alphabetical Order

No.	Latin Name	English Name
1	Andromeda	Andromeda
2	Antlia	Air Pump
3	Apus	Bird of Paradise
4	Aquarius	Water Bearer
5	Aquila	Eagle
6	Ara	Altar
7	Aries	Ram
8	Auriga	Charioteer
9	Boötes	Bear Driver
10	Caelum	Burin
11	Camelopardalis	Giraffe
12	Cancer	Crab
13	Canes Venatici	Hunting Dogs
14	Canis Major	Great Dog
15	Canis Minor	Little Dog
16	Capricornus	Sea Goat
17	Carina	Keel
18	Cassiopeia	Cassiopeia
19	Centaurus	Centaur
20	Cepheus	Cepheus
21	Cetus	Whale or Sea Monster
22	Chamaeleon	Chamaeleon
23	Circinus	Drawing Compass
24	Columba	Dove
25	Coma Berenices	Berenice's Hair
26	Corona Australis	Southern Crown
27	Corona Borealis	Northern Crown

No.	Latin Name	English Name
28	Corvus	Crow
29	Crater	Beaker
30	Crux	Southern Cross
31	Cygnus	Swan
32	Delphinus	Dolphin
33	Dorado	Gold Fish
34	Draco	Dragon
35	Equuleus	Little Horse
36	Eridanus	River Eridanus
37	Fornax	Furnace
38	Gemini	Twins
39	Grus	Crane
40	Hercules	Hercules
41	Horologium	Pendulum Clock
42	Hydra	Female Water Snake
43	Hydrus	Male Water Snake
44	Indus	Indian
45	Lacerta	Lizard
46	Leo	Lion
47	Leo Minor	Little Lion
48	Lepus	Hare
49	Libra	Scales
50	Lupus	Wolf
51	Lynx	Lynx
52	Lyra	Vulture or Lute
53	Mensa	Table Mountain
54	Microscopium	Microscope
55	Monoceros	Unicorn
56	Musca	Fly
57	Norma	Carpenter's Square
58	Octans	Octant
59	Ophiuchus	Serpent Bearer
60	Orion	Orion
61	Pavo	Peacock
62	Pegasus	Winged Horse
63	Perseus	Perseus
64	Phoenix	Phoenix

No.	Latin Name	English Name
65	Pictor	Painter's Easel
66	Pisces	Fishes
67	Piscis Austrinus	Southern Fish
68	Puppis	Stern
69	Pyxis	Ship's Compass
70	Reticulum	Net
71	Sagitta	Arrow
72	Sagittarius	Archer
73	Scorpius	Scorpion
74	Sculptor	Sculptor
75	Scutum	Shield
76	Serpens	Serpent
77	Sextans	Sextant
78	Taurus	Bull
79	Telescopium	Telescope
80	Triangulum	Triangle
81	Triangulum Australe	Southern Triangle
82	Tucana	Toucan
83	Ursa Major	Great Bear
84	Ursa Minor	Little Bear
85	Vela	Sail
86	Virgo	Virgin
87	Volans	Flying Fish
88	Vulpecula	Little Fox

Appendix II

The Twenty-Two Brightest Stars

No.	Name	Constellation	Magnitude	Color
1.	Sun		-26	white
2.	Sirius	Canis Major	-1.4	blue-white
3.	Canopus	Carina	-0.7	yellow-white
4.	Rigil Kentaurus	Centaurus	-0.2	yellow-orange
5.	Arcturus	Boötes	-0.0	orange
6.	Vega	Lyra	-0.0	blue-white
7.	Capella	Auriga	0.1	yellow
8.	Rigel	Orion	0.1	blue-white
9.	Procyon	Canis Minor	0.3	yellow-white
10.	Achernar	Eridanus	0.4	blue
11.	Hadar	Centaurus	0.6	blue
12.	Betelgeuse	Orion	0.6	red
13.	Altair	Aquila	0.7	yellow-white
14.	Aldebaran	Taurus	0.8	orange
15.	Acrux	Crux	0.8	blue
16.	Antares	Scorpius	0.8	red
17.	Spica	Virgo	0.9	blue
18.	Pollux	Gemini	1.1	yellow
19.	Fomalhaut	Piscis Austrinis	1.1	blue-white
20.	Deneb	Cygnus	1.2	white
21.	Mimosa	Crux	1.2	blue
22.	Regulus	Leo	1.3	blue-white

Appendix III

The Major Meteor Showers

Peak of Shower	Name of Shower	Radiant	Maximum Rate	Color/Speed
Jan 3	Quadrantids	Boötes	20-80	blue medium
Apr 21-22	April Lyrids	Lyra	5-15	white medium
May 4-5	Eta Aquarids	Aquarius	10-40	yellow swift
June 15	June Lyrids	Lyra	8-12	blue medium
June 20	Ophiuchids	Ophiuchus	8-20	white slow
July 10	Capricornids	Capricornus	5-30	yellow slow
July 28	Delta Aquarids	Aquarius	10-35	yellow medium
Aug 12	Perseids	Perseus	40-100	yellow swift
Oct 7	Draconids	Draco	7-10	yellow slow
Oct 21	Orionids	Orion	10-70	varies slow
Nov 3-4	Taurids	Taurus	5-12	white slow
Nov 17-18	Leonids	Leo	10-100	green swift
Dec 13-14	Geminids	Gemini	50-80	yellow medium
Dec 22	Ursids	Canis Minor	10-15	faint medium

Appendix IV

The Greek Alphabet

Letter Name	Lower Case Letter
Alpha	α
Beta	β
Gamma	γ
Delta	δ
Epsilon	ε
Zeta	ζ
Eta	ε
Theta	θ
Iota	ι
Kappa	κ
Lambda	λ
Mu	μ
Nu	ν
Xi	ξ
Omicron	o
Pi	π
Rho	ρ
Sigma	σ
Tau	τ
Upsilon	υ
Phi	φ
Chi	χ
Psi	ψ
Omega	ϖ

Appendix V

What's Going On In The Sky

*T*here are a number of fine observing guides available to supplement this stargazing story guide. The author would like to recommend "Binocular Astronomy" by Craig Crosson and Wil Tirion, published by Willmann-Bell, Inc., Virginia, 1993, which helps the skywatcher advance his eye and mind with elementary astronomy and more treasures in the sky visible in binoculars.

In addition to this excellent book are two monthly magazines for amateur astronomers. *Sky & Telescope* (49 State Road, Cambridge, MA 02138) tends to be more attuned to the less scientifically-minded amateur, but offers plenty of technical information. *Astronomy* (21027 Crossroads Circle, P.O. Box 1612, Waukesha, WI 53187) publishes articles on all types of astronomical subjects with perhaps more emphasis on astrophotography and on what to observe.

One of the most invaluable tools for stargazers of all levels is the very inexpensive and highly informative *Sky Calendar* published by the Abrams Planetarium, Michigan State University, East Lansing, MI 48824. This one-page calendar shows, with drawings, what is happening in the sky from dusk to dawn, such as: location of the planets and their alignments to stars and other objects; what particularly interesting objects are visible and their location; and suggests simple astronomy projects to sharpen your observing skills. An uncomplicated chart showing the major constellations is included. This, plus little bits of information thrown in here and there, makes it possibly the best buy for any observer.

Astronomy has become such a popular "sport" that merely gazing at random at the sky is not enough. Only a decade ago seeing just the four brightest moons of Jupiter was a thrilling experience. Now a night session is not complete without a look at some of the moons of Saturn or tracking the path of a comet or an asteroid and checking the present brightness of a variable star. In a few centuries we hopefully will be voyaging among them.

Keep your imagination soaring and your eye high!

Notes

1. One light year, the distance that light travels in one year, is 5.8 trillion miles and equals approximately 63,000 astronomical units (AU). An AU is roughly 93 million miles, the distance of the Earth from the Sun. Pluto, the remotest planet, is 40 times more distant from the Sun and thus 40 AU from the Sun. The nearest star, Proxima Centauri, is 4.3 light years away or about 270,000 AU.

2. Meteors are microscopic bits of debris made of rock, dust and water from the tails of comets and from other objects such as asteroids and planets. Every time a comet is near the Sun, it loses tons of this material which the Earth may intersect. When this material enters the Earth's atmosphere, the friction of its passage causes it to burn rapidly, emitting light. it is this light from its disintegration that you see. Listed in Appendix III are the major meteor showers, the constellations from which they radiate, the date and time the shower peaks and the number of meteors predicted during its peak.

3. In the second century B.C. the Greek astronomer Hipparchus devised a system to classify the stars by their brightness. He divided them into six categories, the brightest first magnitude and the faintest sixth. A step of one magnitude is an increase or decrease by a factor of 2 1/2 times; hence, 1st magnitude is 100 times brighter than 6th. After the invention of telescopes, the scale of magnitude was expanded. At the opposite brighter end of the scale, the Sun is rated at magnitude -26; Venus, next brightest, is magnitude -4, and Sirius, the brightest star is magnitude -1.

4. In 1601 Johannes Bayer assigned the Greek alphabet to the stars within a constellation, usually in order of their brightness. Numbers were later added as more stars were catalogued, but the ancient names of the brightest stars continue to be used.

5. In 1781 Charles Messier, a French amateur astronomer and avid comet hunter, got tired of mistaking fuzzy objects for comets and catalogued 109 of them. These Messier objects, as they are called, are nebulae, galaxies or star clusters and each is designated by the letter "M" in front of a number. Many of the objects may appear as smudges or messy blobs, hence the name, "messy object," used in fun throughout the book.

6. NGC stands for New General Catalog. Galaxies, star clusters and nebulae are referred to as deep-sky objects with NGC numbers.

7. Nebulae are clouds of gas fluoresces energized by hot young stars. M42 is a typical emission nebula containing mostly hydrogen, some helium and small amounts of other elements.

8. All stars, particularly the brightest ones, twinkle because their light is refracted or broken up into different wavelengths by the turbulence of Earth's unstable atmosphere that is thickest near the horizon. When you see an object near the horizon that does not twinkle or just slightly fluctuates, then you are looking at a planet that is reflecting sunlight.

BIBLIOGRAPHY

Allen, Richard Hinckley, "Star Names, Their Lore and Meaning," Dover Publications Inc., New York, 1963.

Burnham, Robert, Jr., "Burnham's Celestial Handbook," Three vols., Dover Publications Inc., New York, 1978.

Crossen, Craig and Wil Tirion, "Binocular Astronomy," Willmann-Bell Inc., Virginia, 1991.

Dickinson, Terrance, "'Night Watch," Camden House Publishers, Ltd., Ontario, 1984.

Eicher, David "The Universe From Your Backyard," Kalmbach Publishing Company, Wisconsin, 1988.
"Beyond The Solar System," Kalmbach Publishing Company, Wisconsin, 1992.

Harrington, Phillip S., "Touring The Universe Through Binoculars," John Wiley and Sons, Inc., New York, 1990.

Kunitzsch, Paul and Tim Smart, "Short Guide To Modern Star Names And Their Derivations," Otto Harrassowitz, Wiesbaden, 1986.

Krupp, E. C., "Beyond The Blue Horizon," Harper Collins Publishers, New York, 1991.

Monroe, Jean Guard and Ray A. Williamson, "They Dance In The Sky, Native American Star Myths," Houghton Mifflin Company, Boston, 1987.

Moore, Patrick, "Stargazing. Astronomy Without A Telescope," Barron's Educational Series, Inc, New York, 1985.

Ottewell, Guy, "The Astronomical Companion," Furman University, South Carolina, 1985.

Rey, H. A., "The Stars. A New Way To See Them," Houghton Mifflin Company, Boston, 1976.

Ridpath, Ian, "Star Tales," Universe Books, New York, 1988.

Staal, Julius D. W., "The New Patterns In The Sky, Myths and Legends of the Stars," The McDonald and Woodward Publishing Company, Virginia, 1988.

Index

168